Learn These 14 Candlestick Patterns and you'll Earn Every Day

14 candlestick patterns that provide traders with more than 90% of the trading opportunities from candlestick trading

Disclaimer

This book is for educational purpose only and should not be construed as an offer of advisory services. Nothing in this book should be construed as trade/investment advice or recommendation of any kind. You should not rely on any statement made in this book for trading on any instrument like stocks, futures and commodities. You are solely responsible for your decision to invest or trade in the stock market or buy or sell any specific share. Information presented in this book should not be regarded as a complete analysis of the subject discussed. If you need advice on investment or trading upon which you intend to rely on in the course of your financial, business or legal affairs, you are advised to consult a competent financial advisor/consultant. All trading and investment strategies have the potential for profit as well as loss. You are solely responsible for any of your decision to buy or sell or invest in any stock, futures, commodities or currencies or any such instrument. All expressions of opinion reflect the judgment of the author as on the date of publication and are subject to change. The Publisher and the Author accept no liability for any loss or damage of any kind that may result from your trading and investment in stocks, futures, commodities and forex markets.

Contents

Conclusion

PART I

i. What are Candlestick Patterns?

Understanding technical tools and indicators and their signals makes the difference between winners and losers in a trade. One of the most indispensable technical tools for winning the game is the candlestick chart analysis.

The following is the image of a candlestick chart. It can be seen that the chart is made of bars. These bars are known as candlesticks. Candlestick chart depicts price on the vertical axis and time on the horizontal axis.

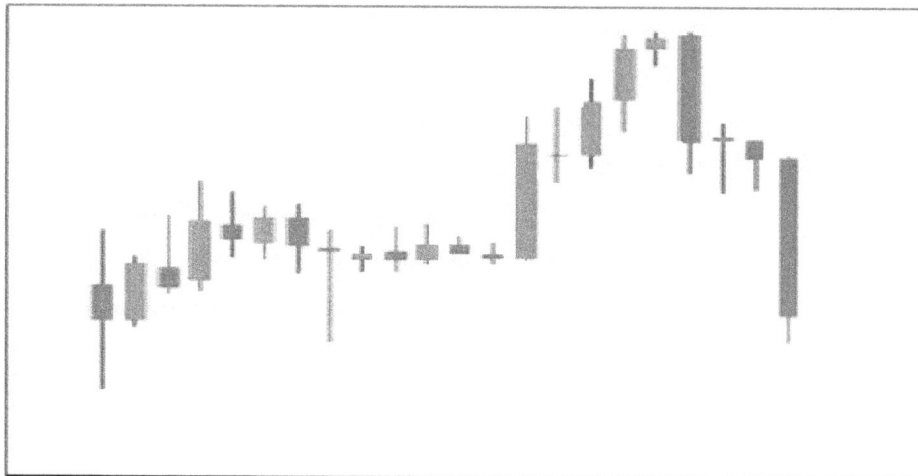

Each candle shows the open, high, low and closing prices for the given period as shown in the following image:

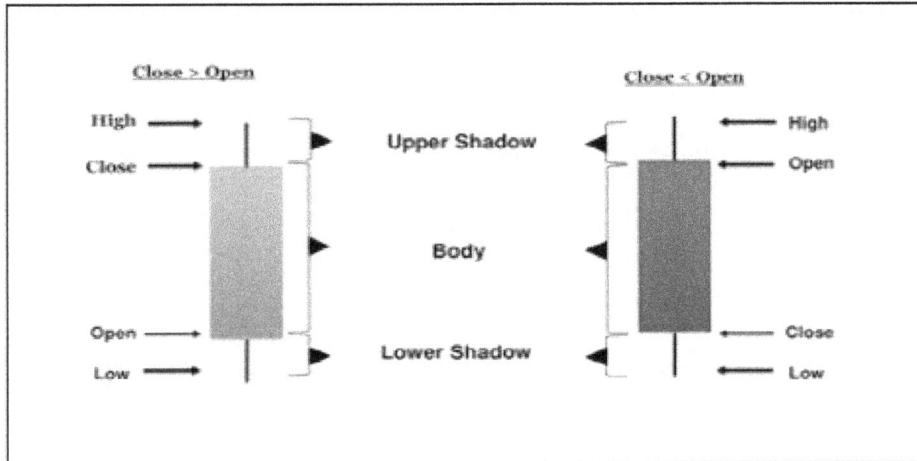

The candlesticks together form certain patterns often and these patterns, with the candles' color scheme, dimensions and body language, convey a lot of information like how price moved during the given period, whether the market is dominated by buyers or sellers and whether the current trend of price is likely to continue or reverse. Hence the trader's ability to identify the patterns promptly and interpret them correctly in a jiffy is a sine qua non for profitable trading.

Many of the candlesticks and candlestick patterns have been named on the basis of what they look like. Examples are Abandoned Baby, Dark Cloud Cover, Dragonfly, Engulfing, Gravestone, Hammer, Inverted Hammer, Shooting Star and Piercing Line.

ii. Anatomy of Candlestick

The data of open, high, low and close construct a candlestick.

Open

The open is the first price traded during the time-frame of the candlestick. The candle will be white as long as the price during the succeeding trades is higher than the open. The candle will be black when the price during the time-frame goes lower than the open.

High Price

This is the highest price traded during the timeframe of the candle. It is indicated by the top edge of the upper shadow. If there is no upper shadow, then the close is the highest price in the case of white candle and the open is the highest price in the case of black candle.

Low Price

This is the lowest price traded during the time-frame of the candle. It is represented by the bottom edge of the lower shadow. If there is no lower shadow, then the lowest price of the given period is the same as the open in the case of a white candle and the close is the lowest price in the case of black candle.

Close

This is the last traded price of the time-frame of the candle. It is this close price which determines the color of the candle. If the last trade of the time-frame closes above the open, the candlestick will be white. If the last trade closes below the open, the candlestick will be black.

Range

This is the difference between the high and the low of the session.

Body

A stock that closes above the open will have a white-bodied candlestick. A stock that closes below the open will have a black-bodied candlestick. The "white" or "black" portion of the candlestick is called "body" (and also as "real body"). In other words, the body of a candlestick represents the difference between the opening price and the closing price of the stock during the given period.

Shadows

The thin lines above and below the body are called shadows, wicks or tails. Top edge of the upper shadow denotes the high and the bottom edge of the lower shadow denotes the low. In other words, shadows "test" a price range and body "confirms" the range for the candle session. Shadow will be long or short depending upon volatility.

Color

Candlesticks are so colored that we will readily know whether the price has risen or declined during the candle's session. Generally, a white (or green) candlestick is used to show that the closing price (or the last traded price) was higher than the open and a black (or red) candlestick is used to show that the closing price(or the last traded price) was lower than the open. Let us use white color to show that the closing price (or the last traded price)was higher than the open and black color to show that the closing price (or the last traded price) was lower than the open.

Time frame

Candlestick charts can be created with appropriate data set containing open, high, low and close for any period like 1-minute, 2-minutes, 15-minutes, 1-hour, 2-hours, 1-day, 1-week and 1-month depending upon the period of price action you like to know. In this book, we refer to candlesticks of 1-day time frame and trading entity of equity stock unless stated otherwise.

iii. Identifying and Interpreting Candlestick Patterns

Candlestick patterns are much useful to predict future price trends. Developing the skill to identify the patterns before trend reversal or break out happens and to interpret the psychology behind the patterns and the implication of each pattern is an indispensable weapon in the arsenal of technical traders.

This chapter tells us how to recognize a candlestick pattern and interpret its implication at just one glance.

Interpreting the "size of the body"

The size of the body of a candlestick body represents the difference between the opening and closing prices. In other words, the size of the body denotes the price gain or loss made by the stock during the given period and thus shows the strength of the movement of price. It shows the extent to which bulls overpowered bears in the case of white candles and bears overpowered bulls in the case of black candles. From the size of the candlestick body, we can gauge the strength of the price direction. The longer the candlestick's body, the stronger is the price momentum.

Long Body indicates heavy trading in the ongoing direction, that is, the session has witnessed strong buying or selling as the case may be. In other words, long body implies heavy commitment by buyers in the case of white candle and by sellers in the case of black candle. That is, a long white candle signifies that the trading session was dominated by bulls and a long black candle signifies that the trading session was dominated by bears.

Small body implies that very little buying and selling happened during the session; neither bulls nor bears could move the price as they liked during the session and prices closed at or near to the open.

Candlestick with no shadow implies a strong trend in a single direction because all the price changes were upward in the case of white candle and downward in the case of black candle without facing rejection at any point of time during the session.

When a large candle closes near the high, it means that buyers were dominating the market and the market trend was strongly upward. When a large candle closes near the low, it means that sellers were influential and carrying the market and the market trend was strongly downward.

Interpreting "change in length" of body

If body becomes longer and shadow becomes smaller, it means that momentum in price is getting accelerated and the current price trend gets stronger.

If body becomes smaller and smaller and shadow becomes longer, it means that momentum in price gets decelerated and the current price trend is reversing.

If the size of the body remains constant, it means that price trend is stable.

If a long white candle suddenly changes into a long black candle and vice versa, it means that very big players are acting on the stock on a large scale or a major development has taken place affecting the stock's value and or demand and supply.

Interpreting shadows

- Shadows indicate the high and low of the candle session. Top edge of the upper shadow represents the high for the period and the bottom edge of the lower shadow represents the low for the period regardless of whether the candle is bullish or bearish.

- Candles with no shadow at all, as already seen, implies a strong trend in a single direction because all the price changes were upward in the case of white candle and downward in the case of black candle without facing rejection at any point of time during the session.

- Length of shadow indicates the extent of price rejection. Long shadow means that there is strong rejection of price. Short shadow means the market is stable.

- If both the shadows are long (when, naturally, body is small), it means that buyers and sellers are equally strong and neither of them is able to gain control and market is volatile and is indecisive as to the future price trend resulting in a no-win situation to both bulls and bears.

- If both the shadows are short, it means that price rejections are weak and market is stable.

- The upper edge of upper shadow may act as a resistance level and the bottom edge of the lower shadow may act as a support level and thus both the edges may be potential trend reversal points.

- Long upper shadow means that buyers were controlling the prices for part of the session but lost control by the end, and then sellers made an impressive comeback and strongly pulled the prices down and caused a weak closing. In other words, long upper shadow and short lower shadow indicate that bears are stronger than the bulls during the session.

- Long lower shadow means that sellers were controlling the prices for part of the session but lost control by the end and then buyers made an impressive comeback and strongly pushed the prices up and caused a strong closing.

- If a candlestick body is much longer than shadows, it means that the trend is strong.

- If a long body is on one side and a short shadow is on the other side and if the body length is still increasing, it means that the price is trending in a single direction and market is healthy.

- If the body length is decreasing and shadow's length is increasing, it means that the trend is weakening.

- If the candlestick body is short and is on one side and a long shadow is on the other side, it indicates price rejection. Such candlestick formations are called Hammer, Inverted Hammer, Hanging Man or Shooting Star depending upon fulfillment of other conditions for the respective patterns.

Interpreting range of the candle

The range of a candle is the distance from the high to the low. The range depicts the extent of volatility of price during the time frame. A wide range means high volatility and a narrow range means low volatility.

Interpreting the color of the candle

We already discussed the color scheme of candlesticks in the chapter on Anatomy of Candlesticks. We saw that a candlestick would be white if the last traded price was higher than the open price and that the candlestick would be black if the last traded price was less than the open. One must note that it is the open of the candle session that is compared with the close of the session in the color scheme of candles unlike in the price quotes of stock exchanges where prices are shown in white color if the closing price (or last traded price) is higher than the previous day's close and vice versa.

iv. Basic Candlestick Formations

The following are a few candlestick formations that represent some basic movements of price that every trader is expected to know:

i) Morubozu

ii) Spinning Top

iii) Doji

The following paragraphs explain about Morubozu and Spinning Top. For Doji, a separate chapter has been devoted under Part II.

i) Morubozu:

Candlesticks that don't have shadows and have only real bodies are called Morubozu. The absence of shadows means that the stock traded strongly in one-way during the entire session. Nowadays, candlesticks with small shadow/shadows are also treated as Morubozu.

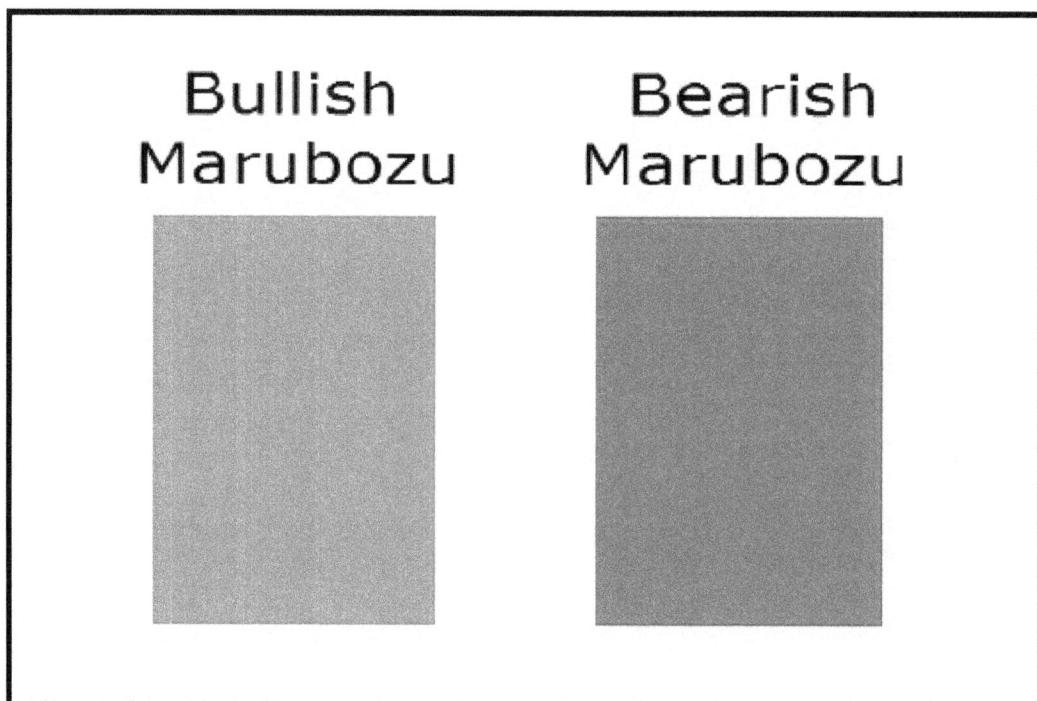

If the Morubozu is white, it means that bulls were dictating to the market from the opening bell to the closing bell and the stock's price was rising throughout the day and its open was the day's low and close was the day's high. If the Morubozu is black, it means that bears were dictating to the market from the opening bell to the closing bell and the stock price was steadily declining from the opening to the closing of the session and its high and low were its open and close respectively.

A white Morubozu occurring in an uptrend may connote continuation of the uptrend, and a white Morubozu occurring in a downtrend may indicate a potential bullish reversal. Likewise, a black Morubozu occurring in a downtrend may connote continuation of the downtrend and a black Morubozu occurring in an uptrend may be a signal of bearish reversal.

Thus Morubozu patterns are highly powerful and their presence matters much to traders in the matter of prediction of future price movements.

ii) Spinning Top

If a candlestick has a long upper shadow, equally long lower shadow and small real body at the center, it is called a spinning top pattern. Color of the real body is not very important.

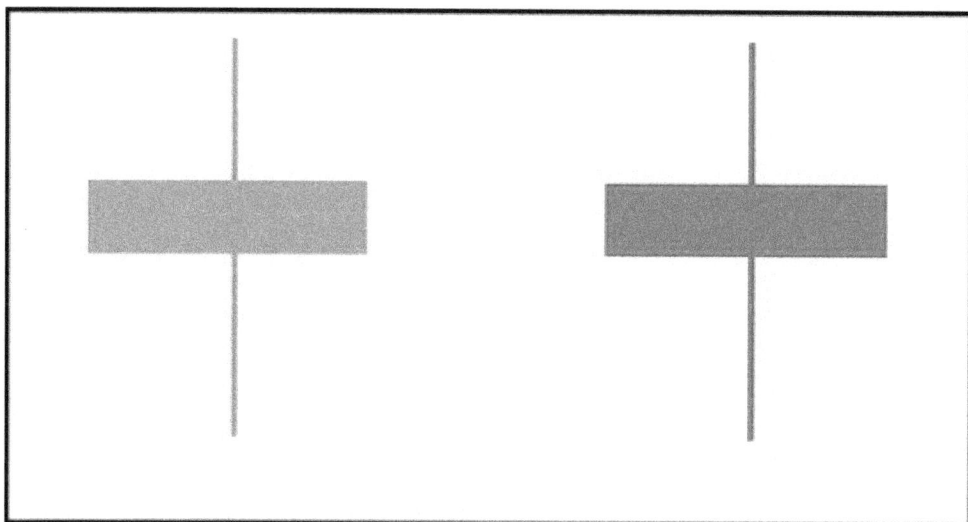

This pattern shows the balance between the sellers and the buyers. The buyers and the sellers took the prices farther from the open as seen from the long lower and upper shadows but neither of them could overpower the other and hence the stock could close only near the open as seen from the small body.

In other words, Spinning Top is an indecision candle and it is alerting the traders that both the bulls and the bears have lost conviction, the ongoing trend is losing momentum and reversal of the trend or range-bound movement is likely.

However, traders make entry only after the subsequent candle confirms trend reversal.

v. Guidelines For Candlestick Trading

- Though a candlestick indicates whether the current market is bullish, bearish or neutral right now, our trade decisions should not be based on that single candlestick alone because such patterns do occur often but the market ignores them and behave indifferently. Trading decisions based on candlestick patterns prove highly successful if confirmed by indicators like RSI and Stochastics, support/resistance levels, moving average crossovers, break of trend lines and high trade volumes.

- A strategy being advocated by many traders is that even if you notice a bullish reversal candlestick, you should look for one or two subsequent candles in the upward direction and enter the trade when the highest price of those candles is reached again.

- Stop-loss is placed at a price little below the lowest price of the candlestick pattern in the case of buy trade and at a price little above the highest price of the pattern in the case of sell trade.

- Determining the target price is important to ensure maximum profit. Some traders fix target price with certain profit percentage in mind. Some wait till the next reversal seems to be around the corner. Some traders put in place trailing stop loss so that the stock will go on earning profit till a reversal triggers stop-loss causing a little and pre-determined sacrifice in profit.

vi. Categories of Candlestick Patterns

Classification of candlesticks as bullish and bearish candlesticks

Market moves upward or downward or consolidates in a trading range. When the price of a stock rises during the trading session, the corresponding candlestick with a price higher than the open is called a bullish candlestick. Likewise, when the price of a stock declines during the session, the corresponding candlestick with a price lower than the open is called bullish candlestick.

When prices move up and down without taking any clear direction, market is said to be in consolidation mode, and the candle of the corresponding session will be having a small body.

The following are the images of a few bullish and bearish candlesticks:

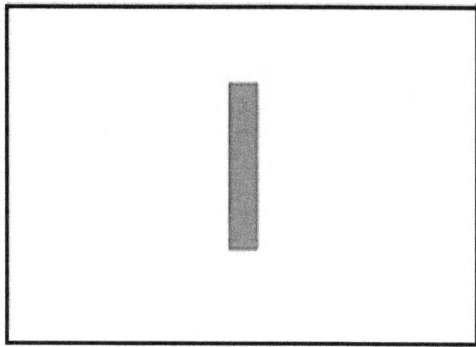

Green Morubozu (Bullish)

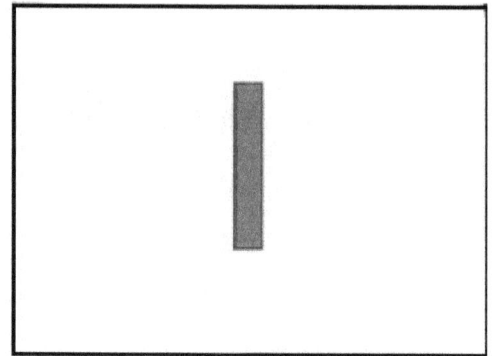

Red Morubozu (Bearish)

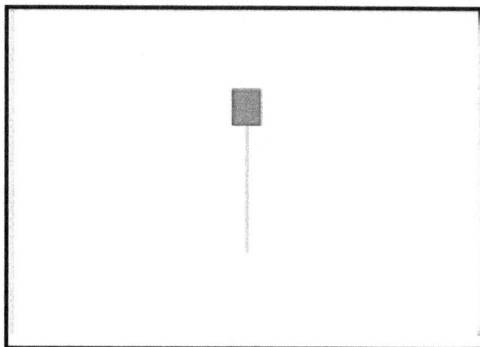

Hammer (Bullish)

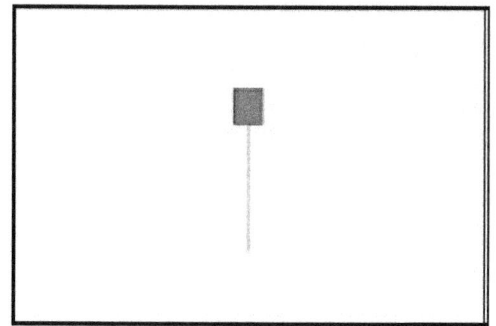

Hanging Man (Bearish)

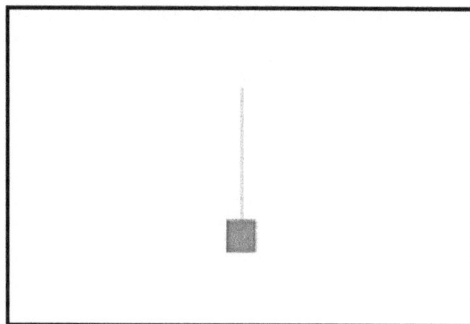

Inverted Hammer (Bullish)

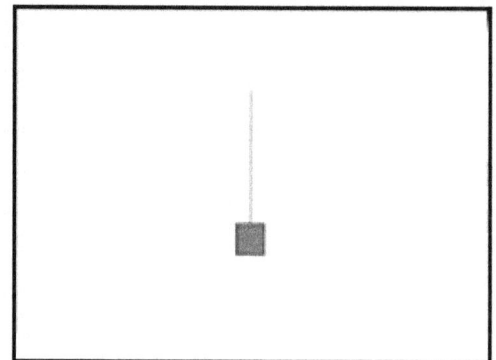

Shooting Star (Bearish)

Classification of candlestick patterns as reversal patterns and continuation patterns

The reversal pattern may occur after a very long uptrend or downtrend that has caused exhaustion and predict the reversal in price direction. The reversal patterns can also occur after news or events that affect the fundamentals of the company, industry or economy. Reversal patterns are further divided into bullish reversal patterns and bearish reversal patterns.

Continuation patterns signal the continuance of the currently prevailing price trend. The continuation patterns are used by traders as a confirmation signal to enter into new trade or to accumulate the asset in the current trend itself. These continuation patterns are subdivided into bullish trend continuation patterns and bearish trend continuation patterns.

Classification of candlestick patterns based on reliability

Candlestick patterns are categorized as highly reliable, moderately reliable and weak depending upon the extent of their reliability to trade measured by the frequency of their occurrence and the accuracy level of their prediction of trend.

Though more than 100 patterns have been identified and named by traders, we have chosen for this book 14 of them that are found to be most reliable to trade because of their frequent occurrence and high level of accuracy in prediction of future movement of prices.

The following chapters guide you on how to spot certain highly reliable candlestick patterns and how to trade them and garner profit.

PART II

1. Hammer

Hammer pattern is a single-candlestick bullish reversal pattern that occurs at the bottom of a downtrend. The pattern occurs frequently. It is easy to identify also. It shows that sellers are able to bring down the price to a new low but the downtrend could not be sustained any longer as strong buying pressure pushes the price up and the market closes near and mostly above the open.

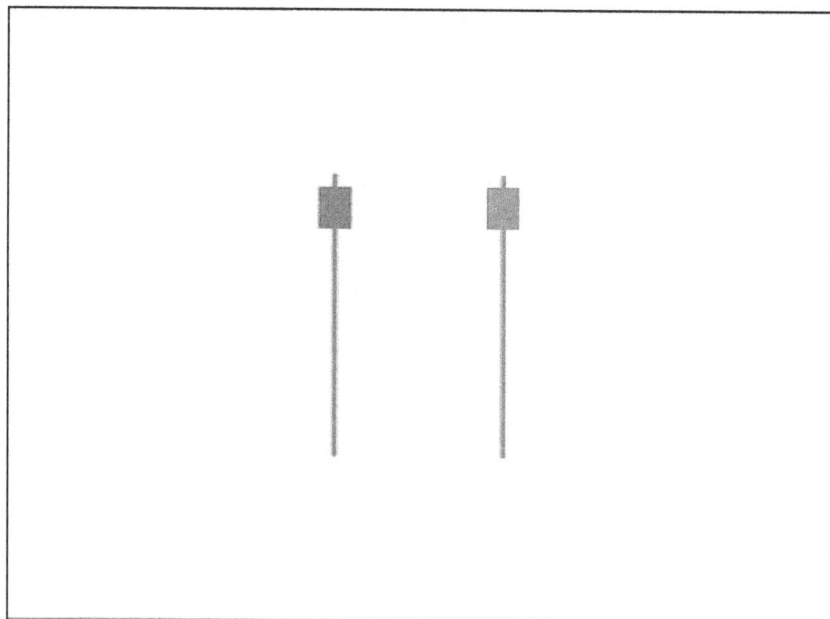

Formation in detail

- The hammer candle, to be an indicator of bullish reversal, should be occurring at the bottom of a downtrend.

- Its body should be short and located at the top of the price range.

- Its upper shadow should ideally be non-existent.

- Its lower shadow should be at least double the length of the body.

- The closing and high positions are similar or the open and high positions are similar connoting that bulls are able to overpower the bears during the time frame.

- The body can be white or black i.e., the close can be a little lower or higher than the open though a white candle is considered to have a more bullish indication and make a stronger pattern.

A candlestick with the same shape but occurring after a bullish trend is not a hammer but is a hanging man pattern.

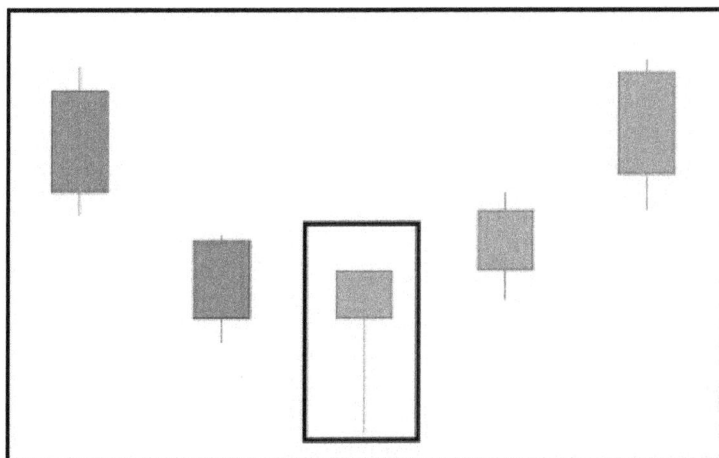

Interpretation:

The Hammer candlestick pattern implies that price moved lower after the open and then ran out of sellers at such low prices and buyers entered because of such low prices and the price closed at or near to the open.

There is little or no upper shadow which means that the market could not trade higher at any point of time during the trading session.

The long lower shadow implies that the price fell to a support level, then bounced upward and went near to the open. In other words, the market's support and resistance levels were being tested by the long lower shadow.

Formation of hammer pattern during downtrend implies that the bottom of the downtrend is nearby and price will start moving up again.

How to trade:

Hammer pattern is a signal to prospective buyers to be alert as bullish trend is gaining momentum.

Many traders will buy the next morning itself if the day's open is higher than the hammer day's close.

However majority of traders wait for firm confirmation of bullish trend reversal by way of a few consecutive white candles.

We recommend entry after a close above the real body of the hammer candle preferably supported by increased volume and long-term ascending channel.

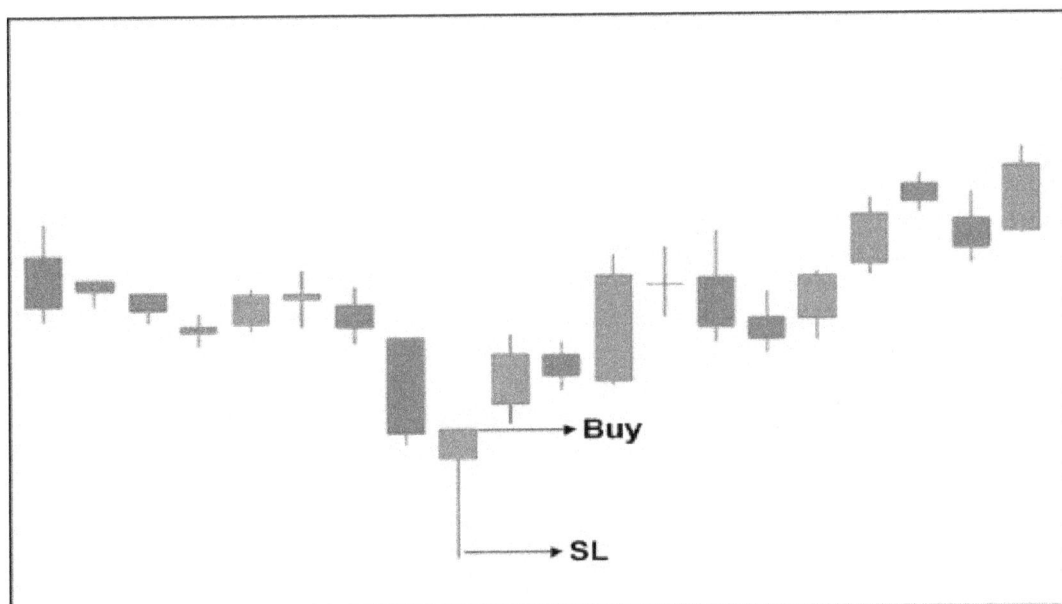

Low of the hammer candlestick is recommended as stop-loss. However, if the lower shadow is very long, stop-loss level will be far away, and hence trigger will entail huge loss. One can, therefore, consider a more conservative stop loss, say, at a level below half of the lower shadow.

Signal strength

- The buy signal of the pattern is stronger when it is formed after a long downtrend in the price.

- The pattern's buy signal will be stronger if the hammer candle is followed by a candle that closes above the opening price of the hammer candle.

- A white-bodied hammer signals a stronger bull market than a black-bodied hammer.

- The longer the lower shadow, the stronger the bullish reversal.

- A hammer candle backed by large volume signals a stronger bull market.

- Gap-up opening and increased volume on the next day make the buy signal stronger.

2. Inverted Hammer

Inverted Hammer pattern is a single candlestick pattern that is similar to Hammer pattern but is inverted. Just like Hammer pattern, this pattern also occurs at the bottom of a trend or during a downtrend.

It forms when the market which is in downtrend rises significantly above the open price during the day and then retreats and trades lower and finally closes near or below the open price.

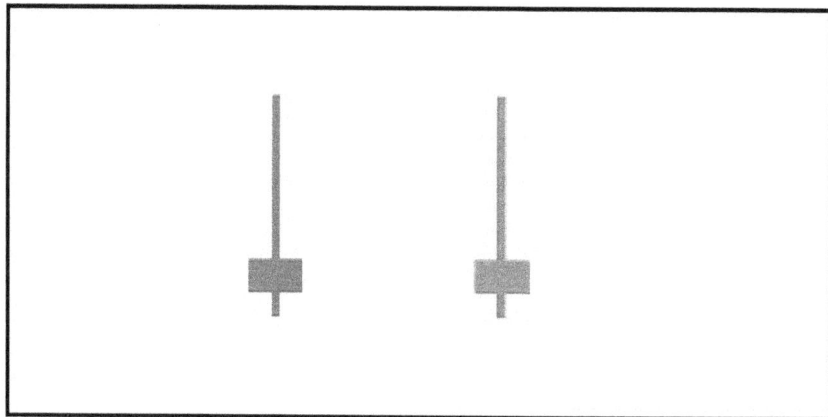

Formation in detail

- Market is in downtrend.

- The candle's color is immaterial i.e., the candle may be white or black.

- The length of the upper shadow of this candle is at least twice the length of the body.

- There is almost no lower shadow.

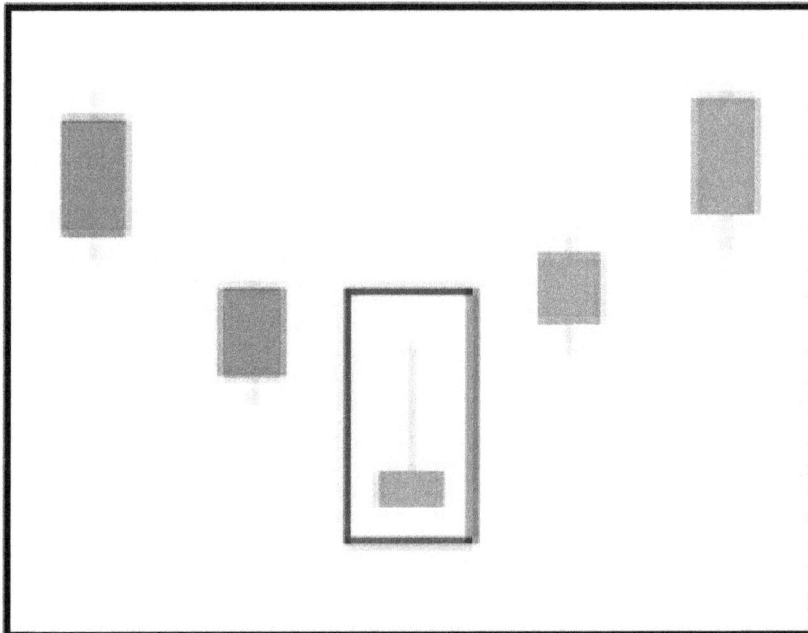

Psychology behind the pattern

The inverted hammer shows that buyers lifted the price significantly (as seen from the long upper shadows) but faced resistance from sellers and the candle eventually closed near where it started. Though bulls might not have become strong enough to close the day higher, it conveys that there is a high chance of buyers gaining control of the market soon causing rally and bears will, therefore, have to stop short selling. Thus it is a good indicator of a bullish reversal of direction.

Trading the Inverted Hammer pattern

Occurrence of this pattern is not necessarily a signal to buy; it is only a signal that the downtrend may reverse and traders may better avoid selling as prices may start rising soon.

However majority of traders enter trade after confirmation by various other parameters like increased volume on the pattern day and the next day, bullish opening and positive volume balance on the next day and a longer term rising trend channel.

Moderately conservative traders wait till the end of the next day and decide to enter trade if the candle of the next day remains bullish throughout the day and closes above the real body of the inverted hammer.

Stop-loss can be the low of the Inverted Hammer in both the above cases.

Very conservative traders enter trade only if the following day's candle closes above the pattern high.

In such cases, stop loss at the low of the pattern candle may be far and may entail a big amount of loss if triggered, and hence stop loss can be fixed at the middle point of the upper shadow.

Determinants of the strength of the signal

- The longer the upper shadow, the more likely the trend reversal.

- The larger the volume on the pattern day, the more likely the trend reversal.

- Though color of the Inverted Hammer candle is immaterial, a white-bodied Inverted Hammer candle i.e., bullish candle ensures high probability of trend reversal.

3. Hanging Man

Appearance of a hanging man pattern while price is in uptrend indicates that sellers are getting stronger than the buyers and hence further price movement is weakening and the uptrend is reaching the top or resistance zone and is probably coming to end.

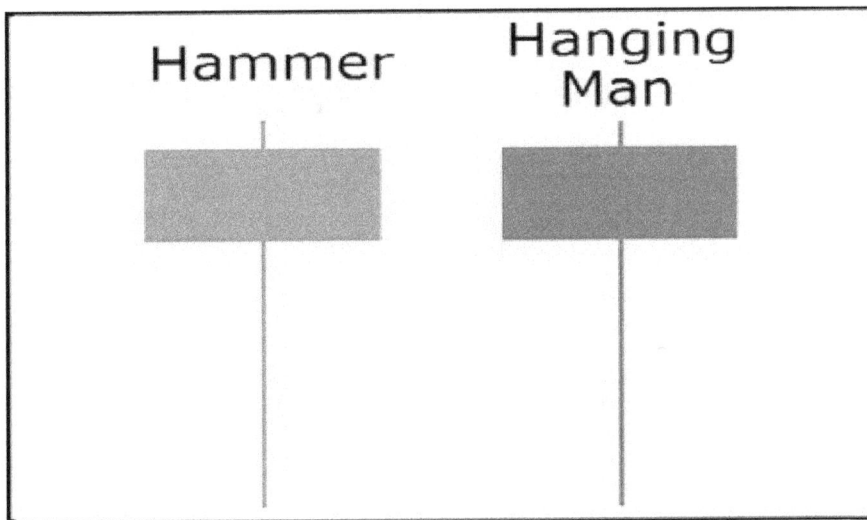

Formation in detail

- The market is in uptrend.

- The candle has a small body (i.e., its close is near the open).

- It has a long lower shadow whose length is at least twice the length of the body. It means that the small body is at the top of the trading range.

- There is almost no upper shadow, which indicates that market could not succeed to trade higher at any point of time that day.

- Color of the body is immaterial. The important thing is that the real body is relatively small compared with the lower shadow.

  The Hanging Man candlestick looks like a hanging man, and hence the name.

The psychology behind the Hanging Man pattern

The long lower shadow implies that sellers entered the market and brought down the price; subsequently, buyers lifted the price but were losing the strength to hold the price higher and consequently the price could reach near to the open only. Little or no upper shadow implies that market could not trade higher at any point of time during the session. Sellers' display of so much selling pressure after a rally shook the confidence of buyers, and buying momentum started to weaken.

If the subsequent candle is black, it is a confirmation that the market has been taken over by bears and the Hanging Man candle's effectiveness as a bearish reversal pattern gets validated.

How to trade

Traders treat the appearance of this pattern mostly as an alert to square off their long position and to go for short-selling.

However, you must always keep in mind the fact that confirmation is always essential for trading based on single-candlestick patterns and this pattern is not an exception to this trading guideline.

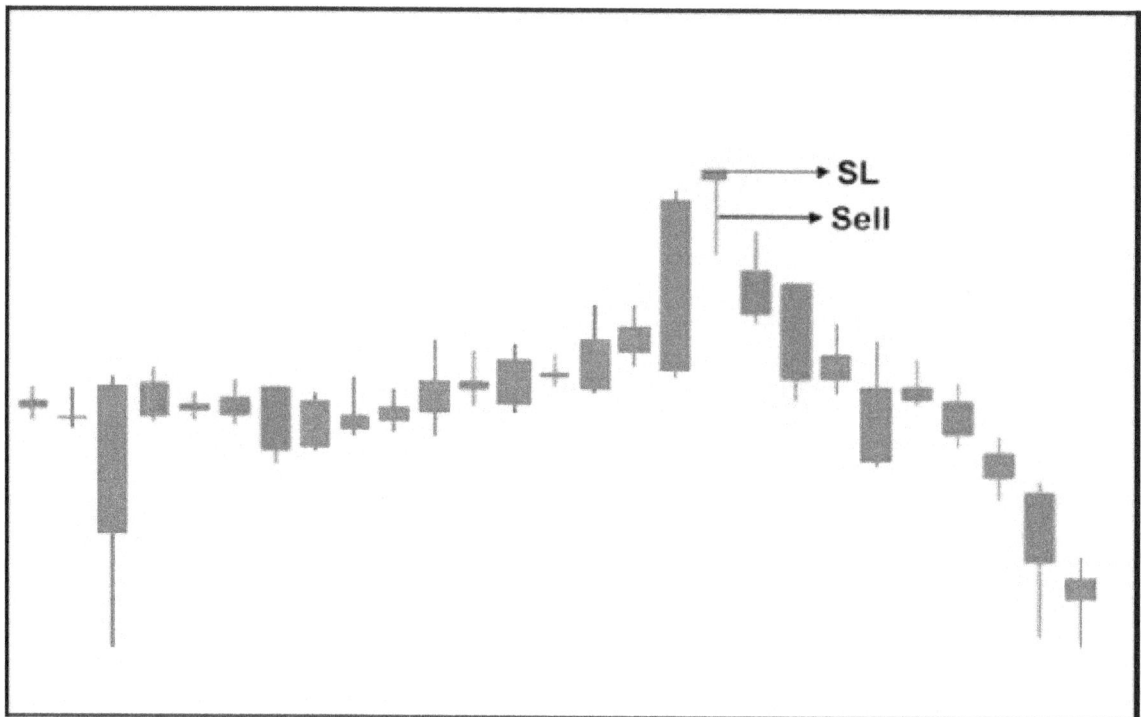

A hanging man pattern that witnesses high volume and long lower shadow followed by a bearish day has the best chance of seeing the prices moving lower. Such conditions provide opportunities to exit long positions and even to go short expecting price decline.

Sell when prices cross below the midpoint of the Hanging Man's lower shadow.

Some like to go short near the close of the bearish day that is succeeding the hanging man.

Those with high level of risk appetite go short near the close of the Hanging Man candlestick or the open of the next candlestick.

The Stop-loss level will be the high of the Hanging Man candlestick.

If a hanging man appears when the price is in uptrend, stop buying and close long positions as the prices will probably start falling.

Magnitude of strength of the signal of the Hanging Man pattern:

- Though the candle can be of any color, the signal will be stronger if the candle is black i.e., bearish.

- The longer the lower shadow, the more effective is the pattern as a game-changer.

- The market that witnesses heavier trading volumes on the day of the Hanging Man pattern have more chances of seeing prices moving lower than that with lower volumes.

- It is not uncommon to see prices continuing the up move despite the appearance of Hanging Man candlestick as the pattern is not a strong indicator of trend reversal unless duly supported by higher volume on the day of the Hanging Man pattern or gap-down opening or steep fall in the next day.

Similarity with other patterns

Two patterns viz., Shooting Star and Hammer look like Hanging Man.

Hanging Man vs Shooting Star

Both the Hanging Man and the Shooting Star patterns occur near the top of an uptrend and both of them indicate fall in prices. Both the candlestick patterns have small real bodies and long shadows that are at least two times the height of the real bodies. The difference between the two patterns is that the real body of a hanging man is at or near the top of the candle while the body of a shooting star is at or near the bottom of the candle. Both the patterns have small real bodies and naturally have long shadows- Hanging Man with long lower shadow and Shooting Star with long upper shadow.

Hanging Man vs Hammer

Both the patterns have small real bodies at the top and long lower shadows that are at least two times the height of the real bodies. The difference between the two is that hanging man is a bearish candle i.e., black, occurring at the top of an upward trend indicating a bearish reversal while hammer is a bullish candle i.e., white, occurring at the bottom of a downtrend indicating a bullish reversal.

4. Shooting Star

Shooting Star is one of the highly reliable bearish candlestick patterns. It signifies that price has reached the top of the uptrend and traders are to close buy positions and may consider going short.

The market opens gap up, climbs much higher intraday and then reverses and closes near the open or lower. Its structure will be as follows:

- It is a bearish reversal pattern that occurs at the top of an uptrend.

- It has a small body near or at the bottom, a long upper shadow at least twice the length of the body and almost no lower shadow.

- The candle may be white or black.

We can understand from the above structure that a Shooting Star forms when the low, open and close are near to each other.

The shape of a Shooting Star candle is the same as that of an Inverted Hammer but the Shooting Star forms in an uptrend while the Inverted Hammer forms in a downtrend.

The shape of the candle looks like a 'shooting star', a meteor falling to the ground, and hence the name.

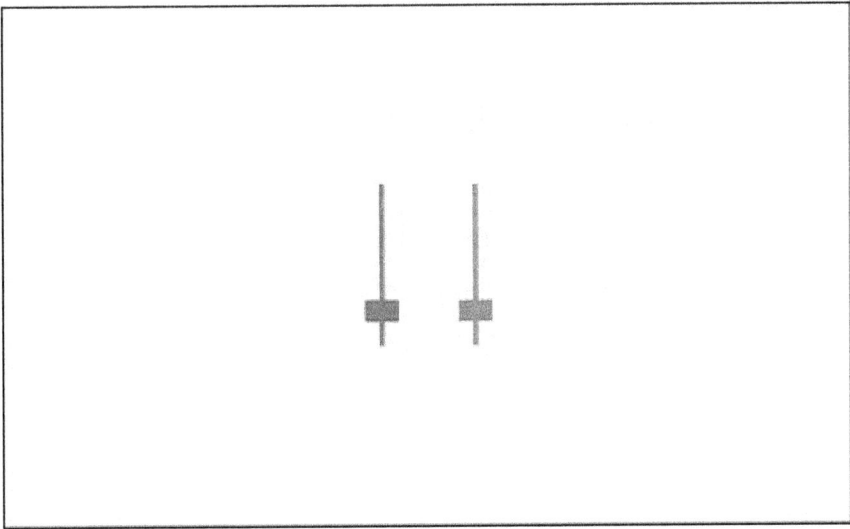

Psychology behind Shooting Star Pattern

The long upper shadow and the small body at the bottom and no or small lower shadow imply that buyers were attempting to lift the market to an extremely high but the market met resistance and bears entered and brought down the prices.

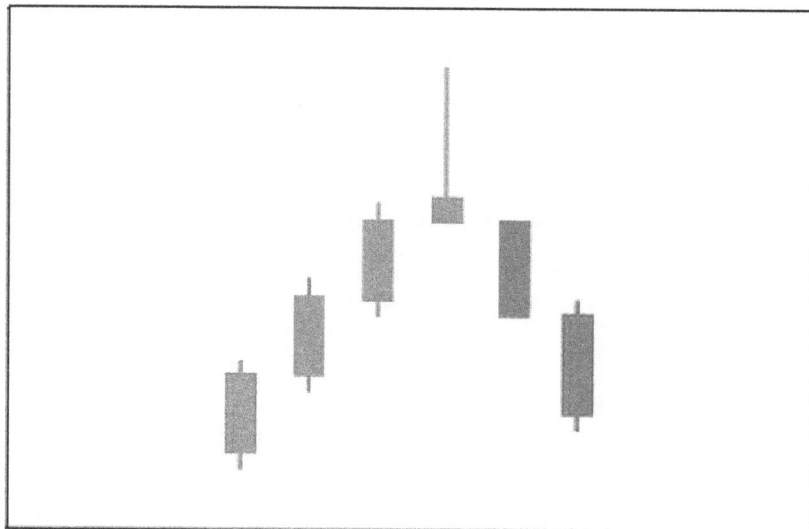

How to trade

Sell when price falls below the low of the pattern. The high of the pattern may be considered the stop loss level.

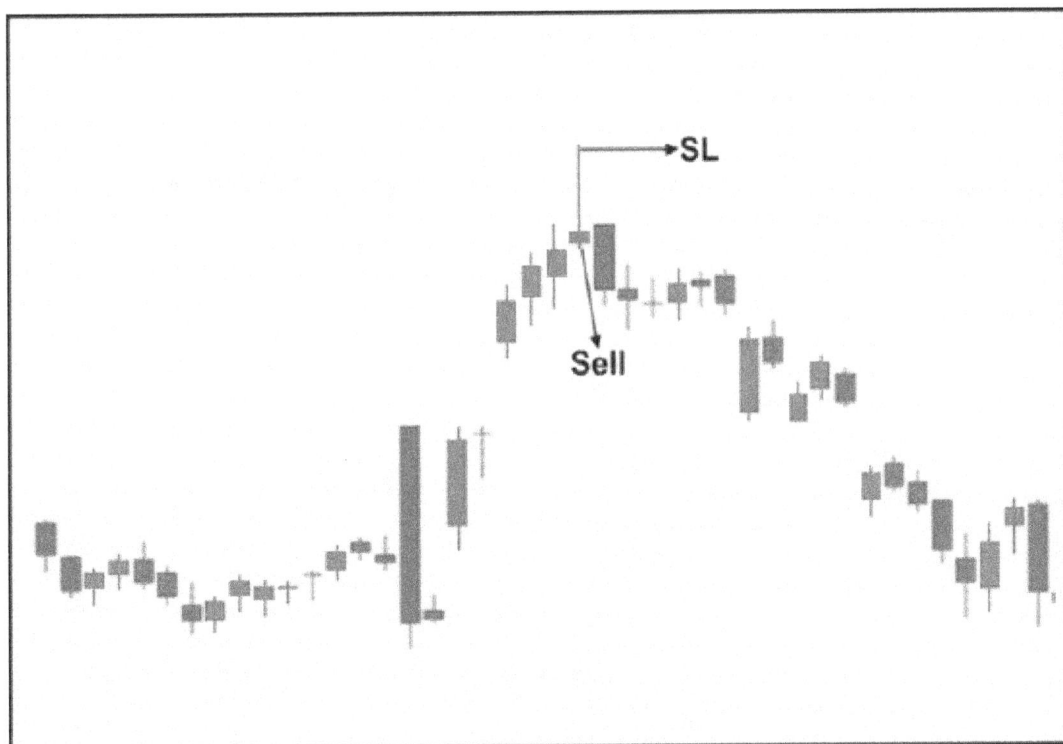

However ensure that support and resistance levels, relative movements of moving averages, overbought readings of indicators like RSI and Stochastics and volume indicators are not against the trade decision.

Magnitude of the strength of the pattern's signal

- A Shooting Star candlestick pattern gets validated as a bearish reversal signal only if the subsequent candlestick is black, i.e., bearish.

- If the pattern forms near resistance zone, its signal of bearish reversal will prove to be highly reliable.

- Though the candle can be of any color, the signal will be forceful if the candle is black, i.e., if the candle closes lower than the open.

- The closer the close and the low, the more probable and forceful the bearish trend reversal.

- A gap-up opening of the pattern justifies expecting a more probable trend reversal.

5. Doji Candlestick

Formation

Doji candlestick is formed when bears try to pull down prices as much as possible while bulls try to push up the prices to the extent possible to them and ultimately the price closes at or near the open without taking any ostensible direction. Since open and close are almost the same, Doji has a small or non-existent body and hence looks like a cross, inverted cross or plus sign.

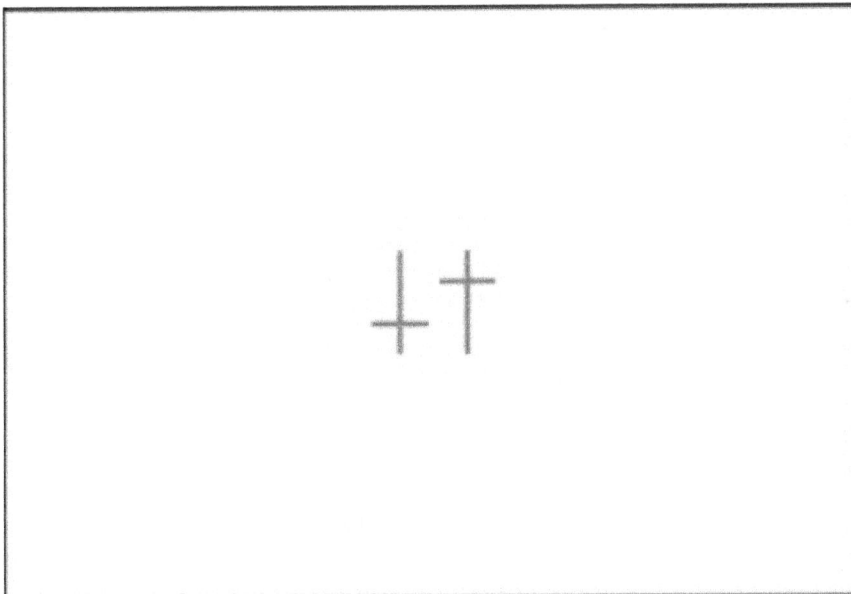

The Psychology Behind Doji Pattern:

Doji implies that indecision is prevailing in the market. Market is not sure of its future direction. Momentum in the market is waning, and both bulls and bears are indecisive and at equilibrium and they don't know which direction the market will take now. Doji represents neutrality.

Different types of doji candles

There are different types of doji candles, namely, the common doji, gravestone doji, dragonfly doji, long-legged doji and Four Price doji depending on where the open and the close lines fall and how long the upper and the lower shadows are.

1. Common (Neutral) Doji candlestick Formation:

- Opening and closing prices are the same or almost the same.

- Hence the candle has no real body or only a small real body.

- Color of the candle is immaterial.

- Both the shadows are almost equal in size and hence the candle looks like an addition (+) sign as in the following illustration.

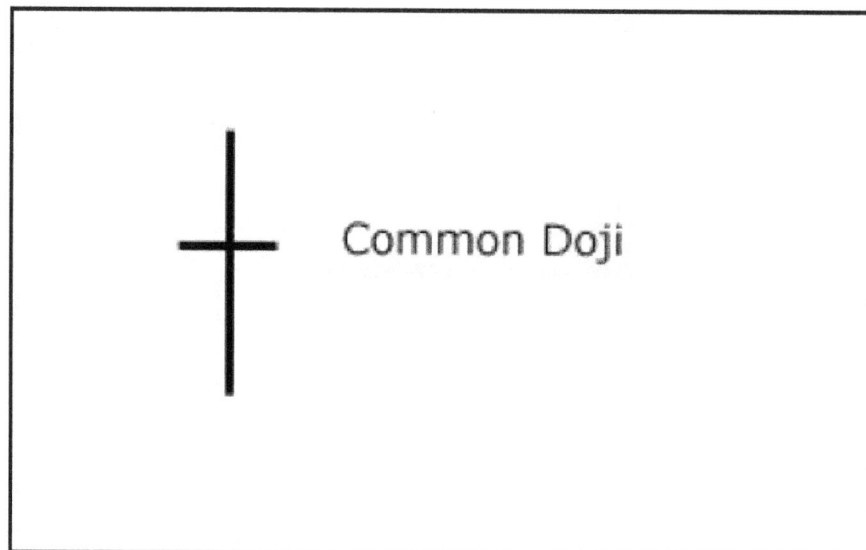

Common Doji

Interpretation:

The session's open and close are the same. It implies that buyers and sellers are of equal strength and market is indecisive in the matter of future direction of market. So next candle's fresh direction will be depending upon some fresh trigger.

2. Dragonfly candlestick

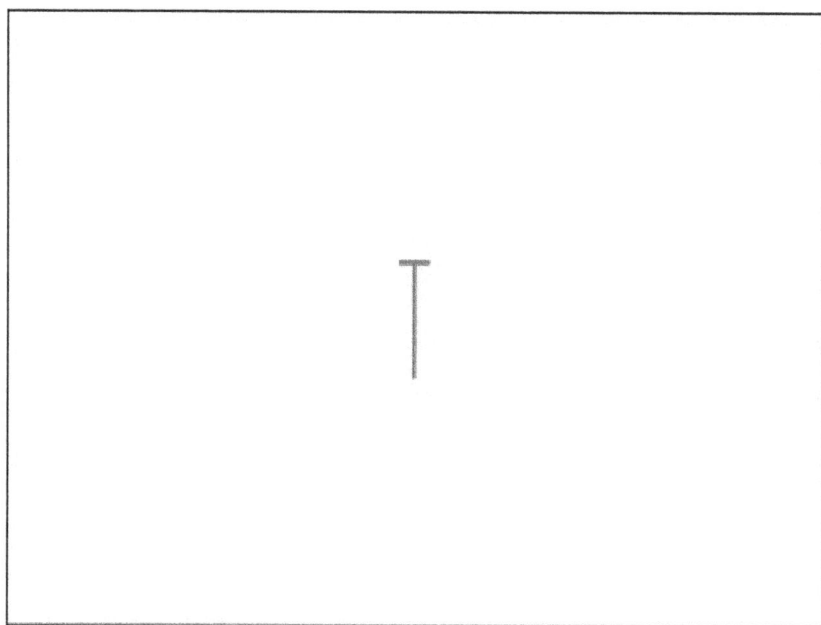

Formation

- Dragonfly is a bullish reversal pattern occurring at the bottom of or during downtrend.

- Its open, close and high of the session are the same or almost the same and hence it looks like it has no body.

- The lower shadow is long implying that the asset had traded at a lower price at some point of time during the session.

- And there is no upper shadow.

Interpretation

- Initially there was aggressive selling and price declined.

- But bulls became active and pushed up the price back to its open.

- Dragonfly Doji Pattern is similar to the Hammer Pattern. The difference between the two is concerning body. In the case of Dragonfly Doji Pattern, the opening and closing prices are identical and there is no real body while Hammer Pattern has a small real body at the upper end of the trading range.

3. Gravestone Doji candlestick

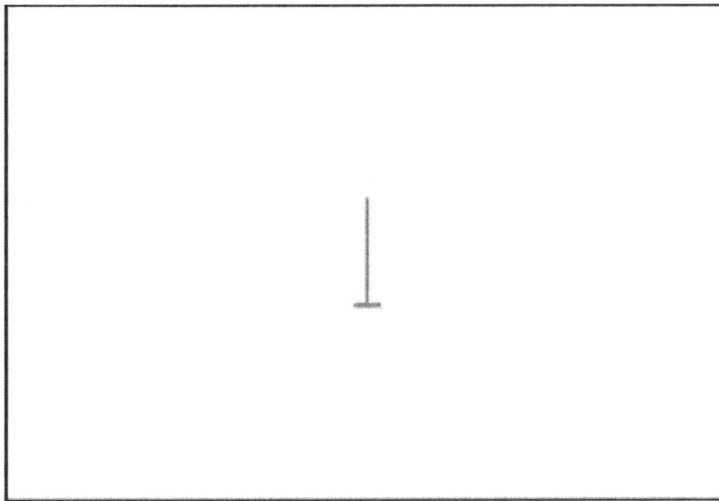

A gravestone doji is a bearish reversal candlestick pattern that is formed when the open, low, and closing prices are all near each other with a long upper shadow, that is, with no real body. The long upper shadow suggests that the bullish advance at the beginning of the session was overcome by bears by the end of the session, which often comes just before a longer-term bearish downtrend.

In essence,

• It has no real body,

• Upper shadow is long and

• There's no lower shadow,

which means that at the beginning of the session, there was strong buying pressure and price rallied and later bears took control of the market and price fell near the open as seen by the upper shadow.

The pattern indicates that the initial upward price trend is likely to reverse and start declining because of the dominance of sellers. If the subsequent candlestick is black, it will mean that bears have succeeded in their efforts, the formation gets validated and the sellers have created a graveyard for the buyers.

Patterns resembling Gravestone Doji:

The opposite of this gravestone doji is the Dragonfly Doji, with body at the top signalling an uptrend. However we must keep in mind the fact that both the patterns should always be confirmed by subsequent candles and also by volume.

Gravestone doji candle looks like a shooting star without a body.

Gravestone doji candle has a long upper shadow and a small body near the bottom of the candle, and thus it is opposite of the hammer.

Trading the Gravestone Doji:

The occurrence of gravestone doji candle can be treated as a signal to book profit if in long position and to go short also.

The pattern is more reliable if it occurs near a resistance level.

Anyway, it will be always prudent to treat doji candles as representing indecision and one should always wait till the next candle, as well as volume, confirm the reversal.

4. Long-legged Doji candlestick (Rickshaw Man)

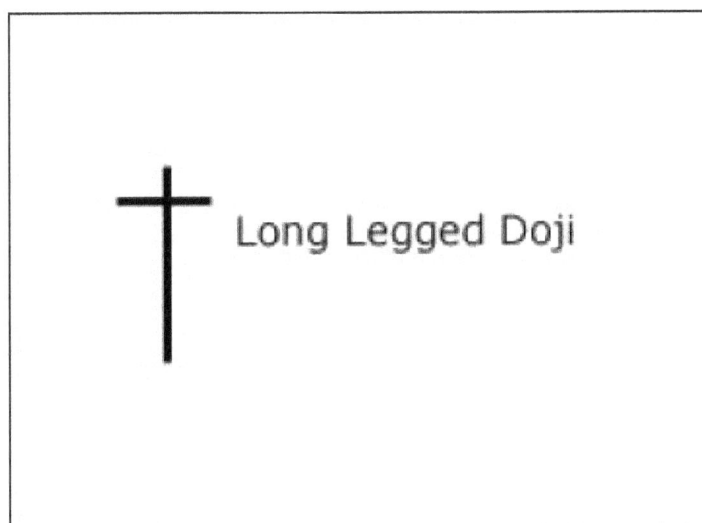

Long Legged Doji

A long-legged Doji is also called a "Rickshaw Man". It is the same as a regular Doji, except that the upper and lower shadows are much longer than in the case of the regular Doji. The longer the shadows, the greater the indecision in the market.

The following is an example of Long-legged Doji formation:

Let us assume that the shares of the company ABC Ltd open at Rs.102. During the course of the trading session, the share touches a high of Rs.107 and a low of Rs.98 and closes at Rs.102.50. This forms a Long-legged Doji.

The Long-legged Doji can be bullish or bearish depending upon the side of the trend where it has formed.

Long-legged doji shows a lot of indecision about the likelihood of the trend continuing.

5. Four Price Doji:

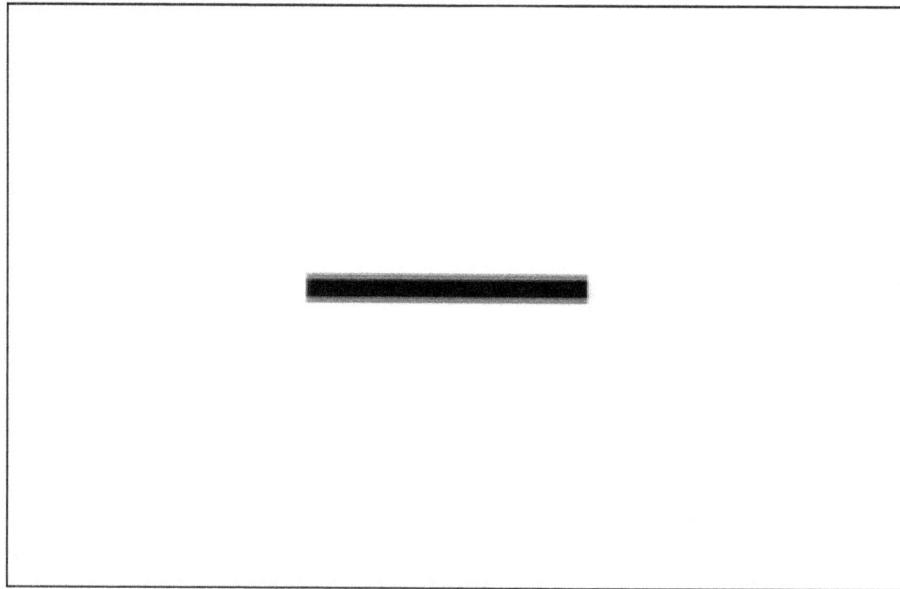

There are some occasions when the asset is traded at the opening price throughout the session. In such cases, the Doji candle is simply a dash without any shadow as seen from the following:

Multi-candle patterns where dojis are present as stars

A single doji is generally a neutral pattern but its relative position at a series of candles provides vital indication in making trade decisions. The following are a few candlestick patterns with doji as a decisive candle:

- **Bullish Trend Doji Star**

- **Bearish Trend Doji Star**

- **Morning Doji Star (dealt with in a separate chapter titled Morning Star)**

- **Evening Doji Star (dealt with in a separate chapter titled Evening Star)**

A doji indicates indecision and a star indicates trend reversal. The above patterns, therefore, usually signal a reversal after a state of indecision. One must, therefore, wait for a confirmation candle before trading a Doji star.

Bullish Doji Star

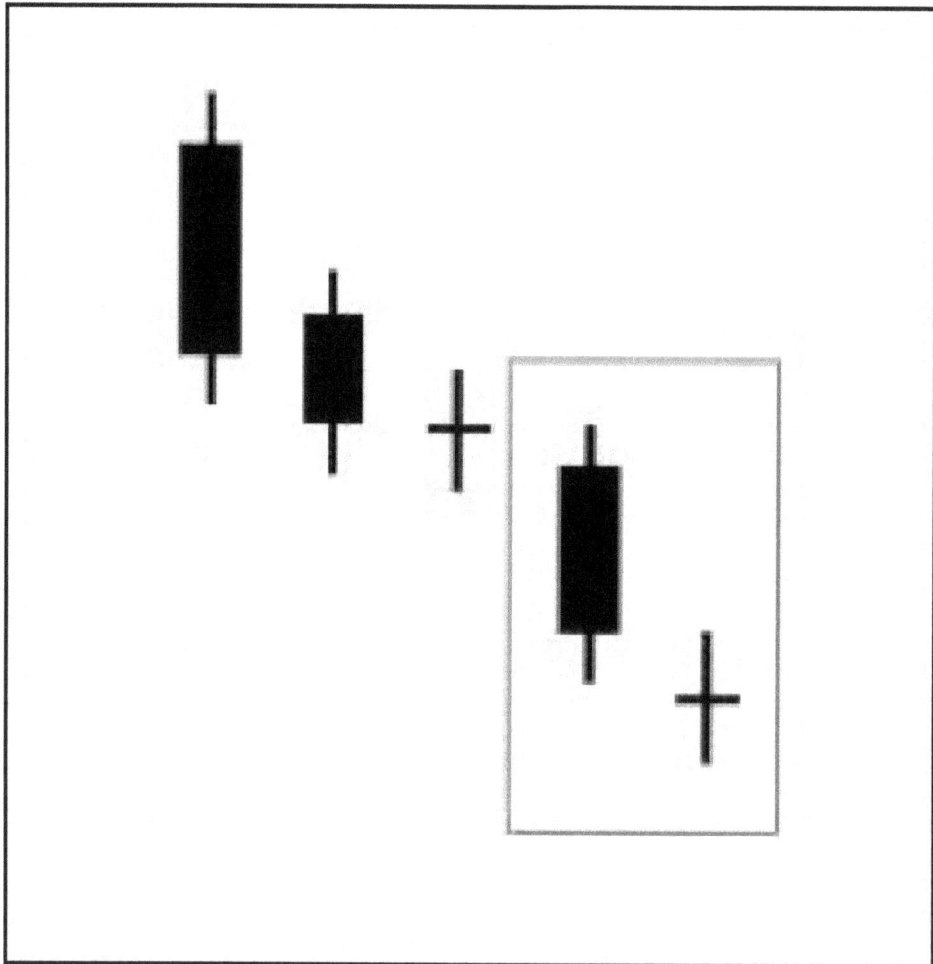

Identification:

- Market is on downtrend.

- The first day is a long black day.

- Second day is a doji that opens gap down from the first day.

- The shadows of this doji are not long.

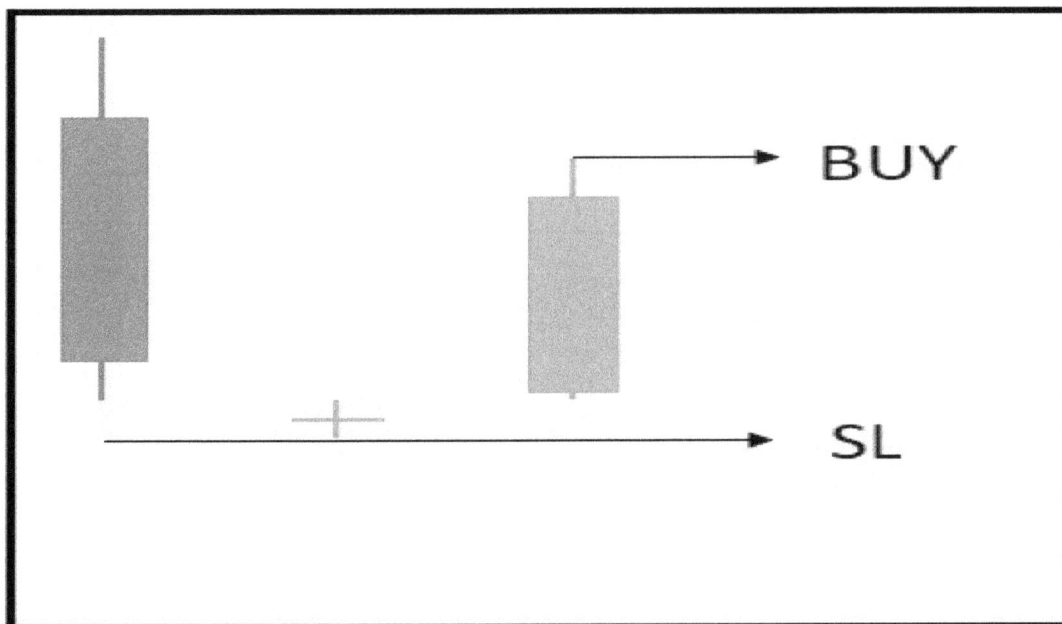

Interpretation:

The market was in strong downtrend during the previous session. Today it opens gap down. Trades are done in a small range. The day's close is nearly the same as open and thus a doji is formed which implies that bulls and bears are in equal control of the market. The confidence of the bears is shattered as the market managed to close near the open. The bearish sentiment is waning. The bears will start covering their shorts if the next day opens higher.

Trading:

Buy when the price crosses the midpoint of the gap between the doji and the previous day's candlestick. Stop-loss can be placed at the lowest point of the two candles.

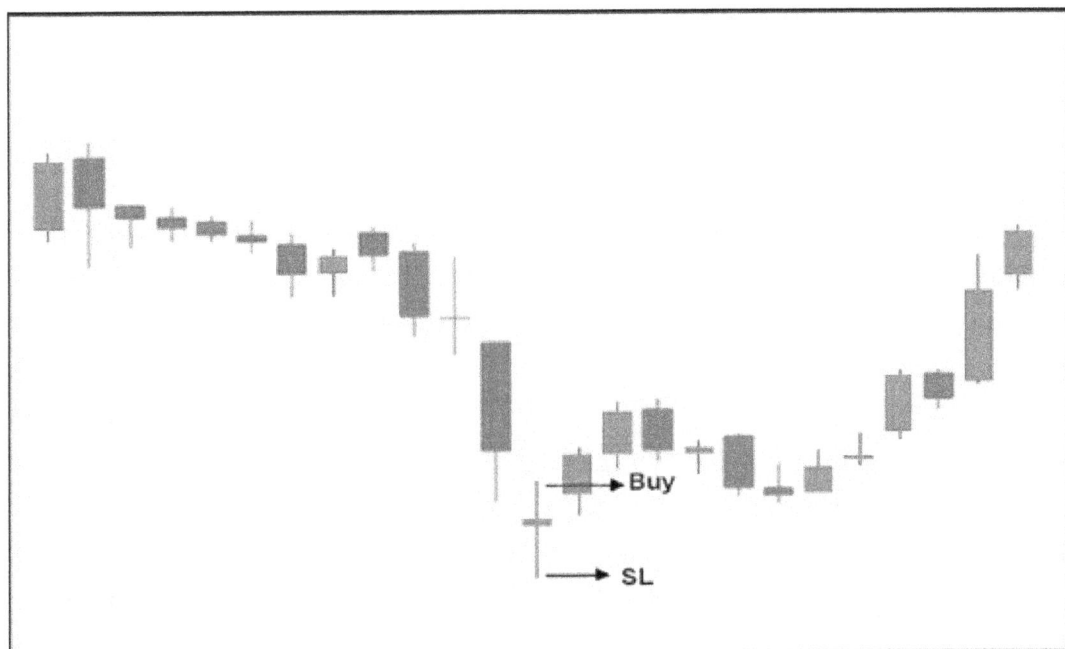

Bearish Trend Doji Star
Formation:

- Existing market trend is upward.

- First day is a long white day.

- Second day is a doji day that opens gap up from the 1st day.

- The shadows of the doji are not very long.

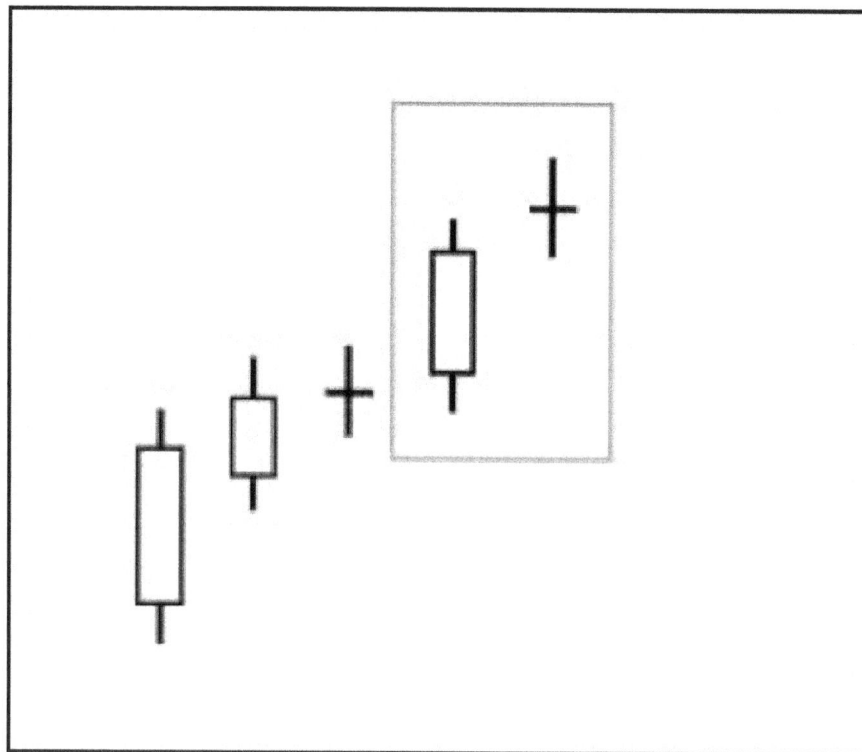

Interpretation:

First day was a strong bullish day. Second day opened and went still higher but bears' sentiment overtook the bulls' sentiment and price fell and closed near the open which shook the confidence of bulls.

Trading:

Profit-booking-spree will be there in the next session if the session opens lower.

The traders who are conservative wait till the completion of a black candle following the doji candle and sell when the price falls below the low of the day after the doji day. Stop-loss will be set a little above the pattern high.

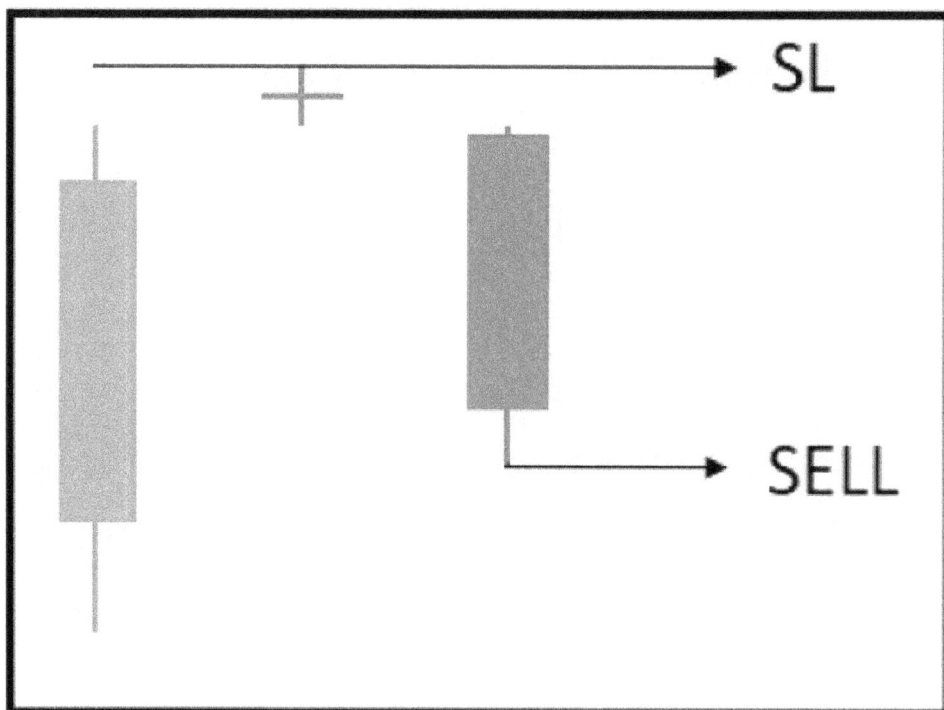

Important guidelines for trading dojis

- Does Doji appear? Don't be excited by the appearance of a doji pattern. Don't rush to make any fresh buy or sell because a doji pattern is not necessarily a trend reversal pattern; the current trend may continue despite the appearance of doji candle as buyers and sellers are at equal strength and market exhibits indecision and neutrality. Treat it like a reversal signal if the trend starts reversing. Treat it as a signal to remain calm and wait if no reversal seems to be in the offing.

- However, the doji may be an indication of weakening of the current trend and you may, therefore, book profit if already in bought or sold position.

- Appearance of doji when the stock is in overbought or oversold condition may be an indication of highly probable trend reversal.

- Appearance of doji in a range-bound market may not carry weight since the market is already indecisive.

- Before acting on the appearance of doji patterns, one must look at momentum indicators like Stochastics, MACD and Williams %R and confirm that market has started showing trend reversal as anticipated.

- When a Doji occurs on your chart, look at the previous candlesticks. If the previous candle is a bearish trend reversal candle-like Shooting Star or Inverted Hammer, you must close all your long positions as bears are likely to start dominating the market. If the previous candle is a bullish reversal candle-like Hammer, you must cover all your short positions as the market is likely to be dominated by bulls.

6. Bullish Engulfing & Bearish Engulfing Patterns

Bullish Engulfing Pattern and Bearish Engulfing Pattern are mirror images of each other-the former is falling and the latter is rising. In Bullish Engulfing Pattern, first body is bearish and second body is bullish. In Bearish Engulfing Pattern, first body is bullish and second body is bearish. In both the patterns, the body of the second day completely engulfs the body of the first day.

Bullish Engulfing

Bullish Engulfing Pattern is a two-candle reversal pattern wherein a white candle closes higher than the opening of the previous day's black candle after opening lower than the close of the previous day's black candle.

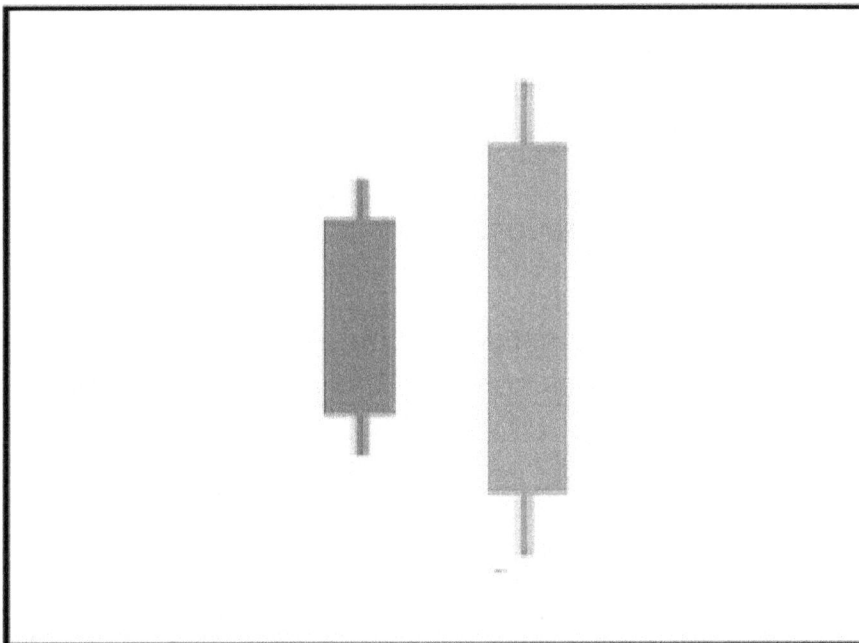

Formation in detail

- The Bullish Engulfing Pattern occurs at the bottom of a downtrend.

- First candle is black.

- Second candle is white.

- The second candle's real body completely engulfs the first candle's real body. That is, the first candle's body is completely inside the second candle's body. In other words, the white candle opens lower than the previous day's close and closes higher than the previous day's open.

- Shadows are not a consideration.

This pattern with a long white candle is considered a bullish reversal pattern if it occurs in downtrend and as continuation pattern if the market is already in uptrend.

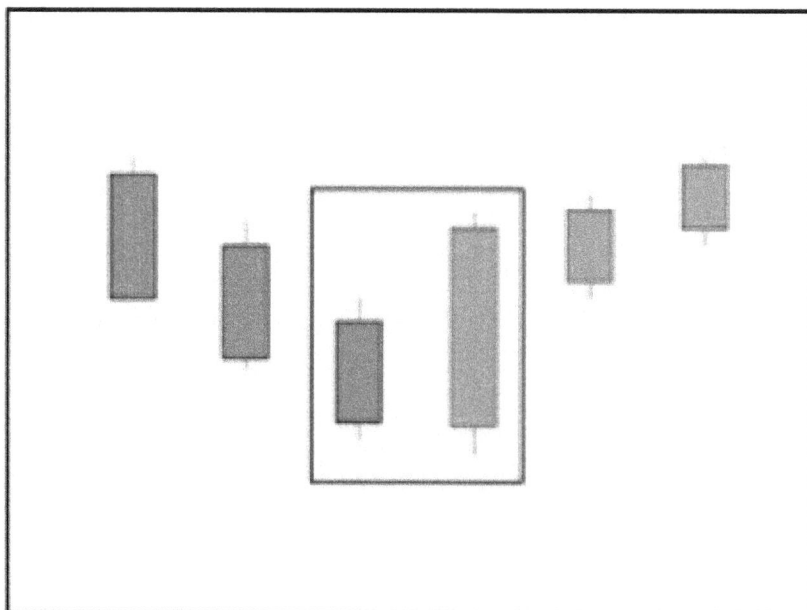

Interpretation of the Bullish Engulfing Pattern

When a market makes a low that is below the previous day's low and closes higher than the previous day's high, it indicates that market is no longer in the control of bears and a powerful trend reversal happens, and hence the market enters into a state of euphoria.

How to trade a Bullish Engulfing Pattern

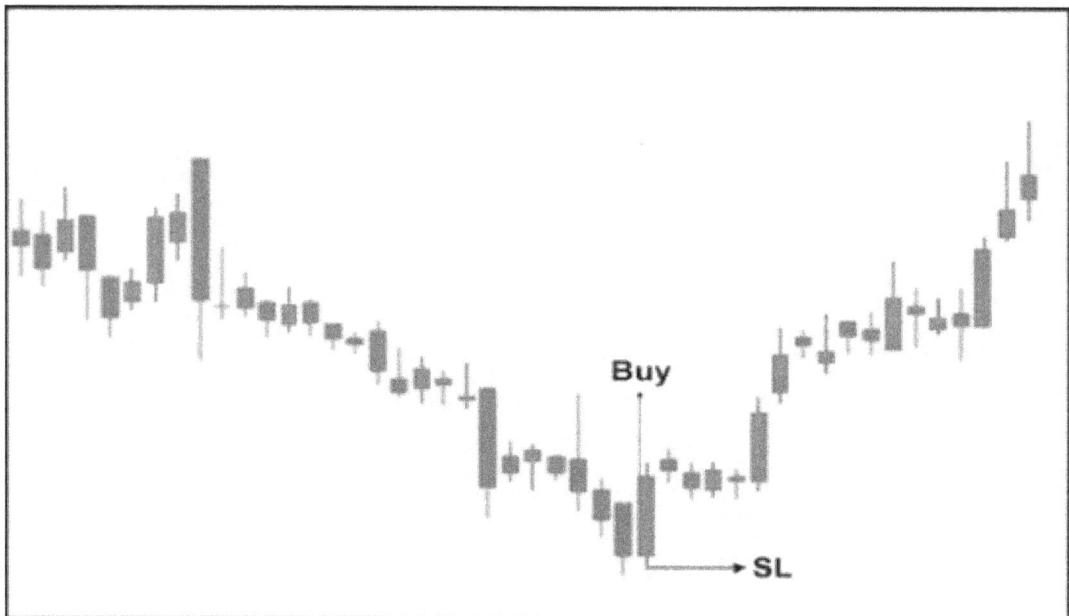

The thumb rule of candlestick trading is to enter the market above the bullish candlestick in a bullish movement and below the bearish candlestick in a bearish movement.

If a Bullish Engulfing Pattern forms during a downtrend, it strongly indicates that the sellers have become exhausted. If the pattern forms during an uptrend, it indicates that a continuation of the bullish trend is likely. We must, therefore, be sure before entering into trade that the present upward move after the Bullish Engulfing Pattern will continue and is not a mere short-stinted momentary jerk caused by a very sharp fall.

Now let us see when to enter the market if a Bullish Engulfing Pattern has formed at the bottom of a downtrend.

Some traders get excited to see the market opening gap down and then rallying to close above the close of the previous day. To derive maximum profit from the reversal of trend, they enter at the close of the second day, of course, after confirming that there is significant increase in volume on the day.

Some traders would like to wait and see how the market opens the day after the engulfing. If the market opens comfortably in white, they infer that the previous day's euphoria still continues, and they go long.

Many customers like to enter the market only after the third day's price crosses above the close of the engulfing day.

More conventional traders like to plunge into the market only after confirming that the third day's candle closes above the high of the engulfing candle.

Anyway, one must confirm before entering into trade that the engulfing pattern is supported by increased volume, longer-term rising trend channel and safely distant resistance zone.

A close below the low of the pattern is recommended as the stop-loss.

Bearish Engulfing Pattern

Formation In Detail

- Bearish Engulfing Pattern is a bearish reversal pattern that occurs at the end of an uptrend.

- First candle is white.

- Second candle is black.

- First candle's body is completely inside the body of the second candle. That is, the first candle's body is fully engulfed by the second candle's body. In other words, the second candle opens higher than the previous day's close and closes lower than the previous day's open.

- Shadows are not a consideration.

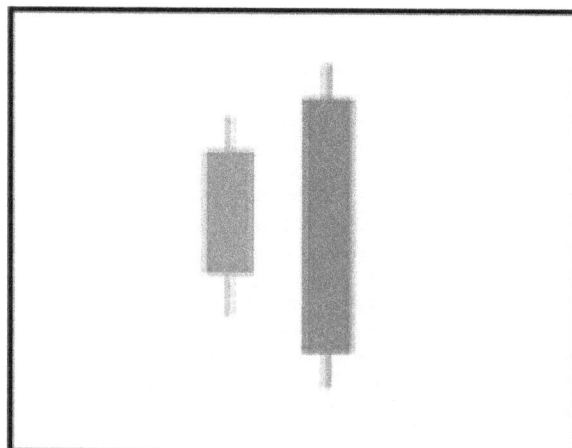

The bearish engulfing pattern can happen at the top of a range or inside a trend. If it happens at the top, it is considered a bearish reversal pattern, and if it occurs during a downtrend, it is considered a continuation pattern. In both the conditions, the pattern signals that further moves will be downward only.

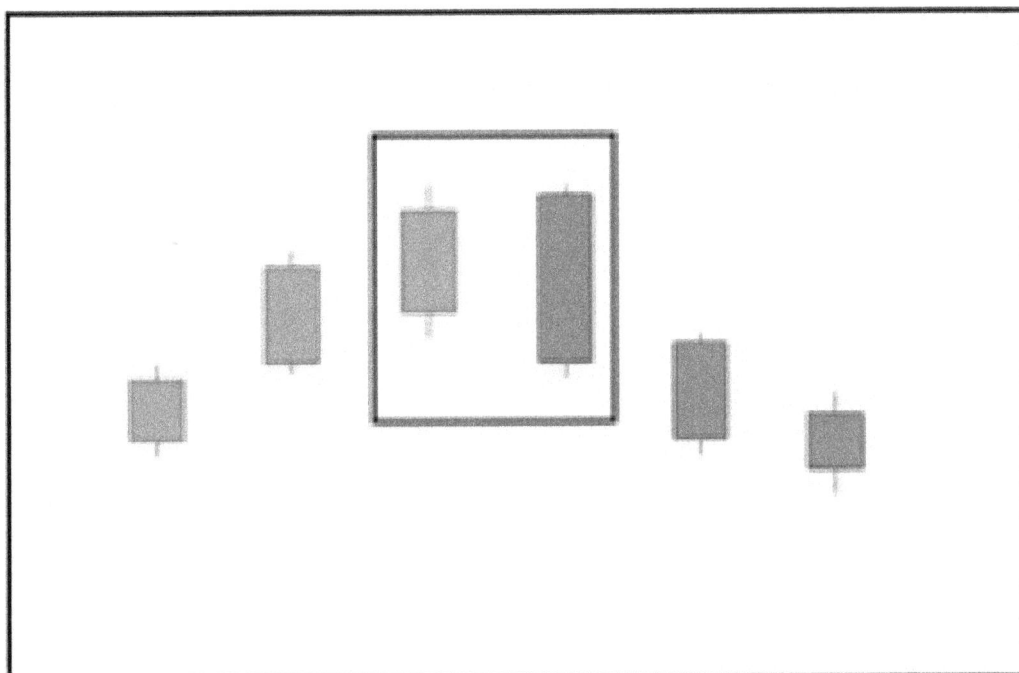

Interpretation:

The second candle rises above the previous day's high, and finding increased selling volume, falls sharply breaking the previous day's low. This may be an indication that a sharp and strong trend reversal has taken place and a sustained downtrend in price is underway.

How To Trade

Traders may go short below the last close or near the succeeding open.

The high point of the candlestick pattern formation is recommended as stop loss.

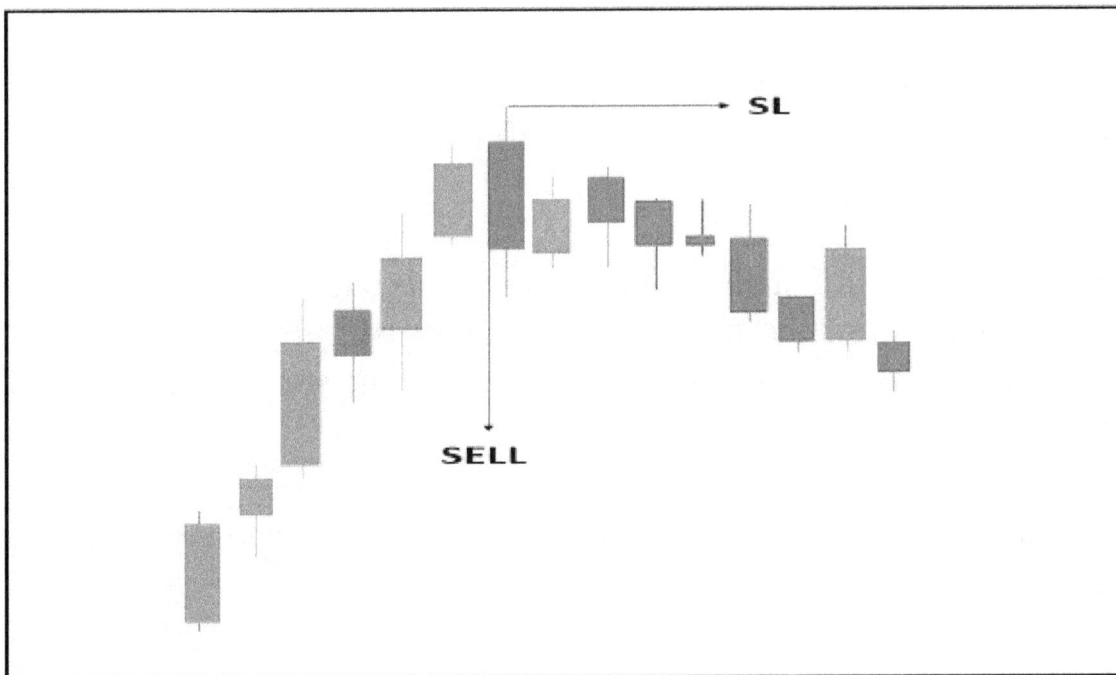

However, it must be understood that the mere presence of an engulfing candle won't justify a decision to take a position. An engulfing candle will be traded only if it forms after an extended move or at a support/resistance zone.

Determinants of signal strength of Engulfing Patterns

A small candle on the first day and a bigger candle on the second day imply that momentum in the trend on the first day was fizzling out and a powerful reversal of trend happened on the second day. In essence, the bigger the difference in the size of the two candles, the stronger the reversal.

If the second candle engulfs not only the body of the first candle but also the shadows of the first candle, the reversal will be stronger.

If the second day's candle engulfs not only the first day's candle but also a few more preceding candles, the reversal signal of the pattern will be stronger.

In the case of Bullish Engulfing, the lower the second candle goes down, the stronger the signal of the trend reversal. Similarly, In the case of Bearish Engulfing, the higher the second candle goes up, the stronger the strength of trend reversal.

The greater the open gaps up or gaps down from the previous close, the stronger the signal of trend reversal.

Higher volume on the second day increases the strength of the signal of trend reversal.

7. Harami & Harami Cross

Harami

Harami candlestick pattern is a two-candle pattern. Harami means 'pregnant' in the Japanese language. The first candle is long and is moving with the market trend. (That is, the color of the first candle is the same as that of the prevailing market trend). The second candle is shorter than the first candle. Its color is opposite to that of the first candle. The second candle's real body is small, and the real body is completely within the real body of the first candle. In other words, the first candle's body fully engulfs the second candle's body like a pregnant mother.

Bullish Harami

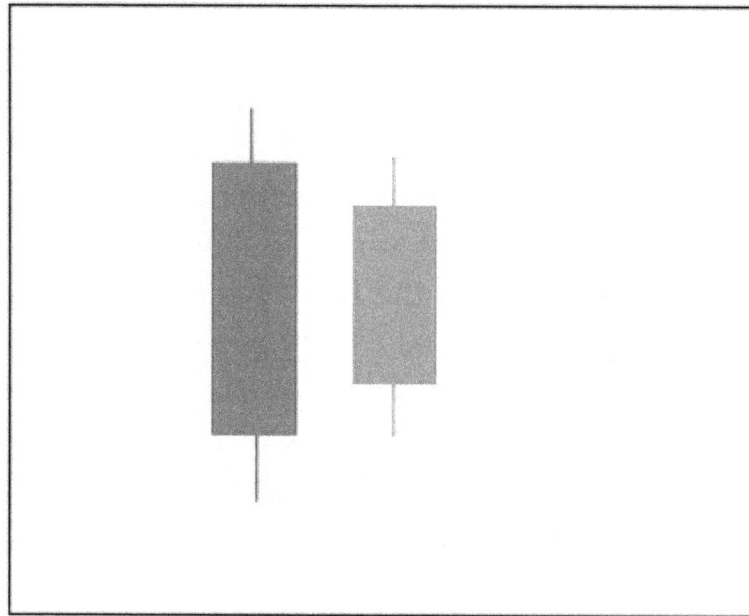

Formation

- Bullish Harami is a trend reversal candlestick pattern that occurs at the end of a downtrend.

- First candle is black and has a large body indicating a high level of selling interest.

- Second candle is white. Its body is completely within the body of the first candle.

Interpretation

The first day was bearish and was witnessing heavy selling and the next day price gapped up (which means that the upward momentum was very strong), was steadily rising and was above the close of the previous day throughout the session. This upward momentum may lead to short-covering which may ultimately lead to rise in price.

How to trade

A buy is recommended when the price crosses above the midpoint of the first candle's body or the last close, whichever is higher. Stop loss will be the lowest point of the pattern.

However, while making a buy decision based on the Bullish Harami pattern, one should always ensure that a support zone is nearby and a resistance zone is not near. Favourable indications by technical indicators like RSI and Stochastics reversing from an oversold zone should also be a major positive factor for buying.

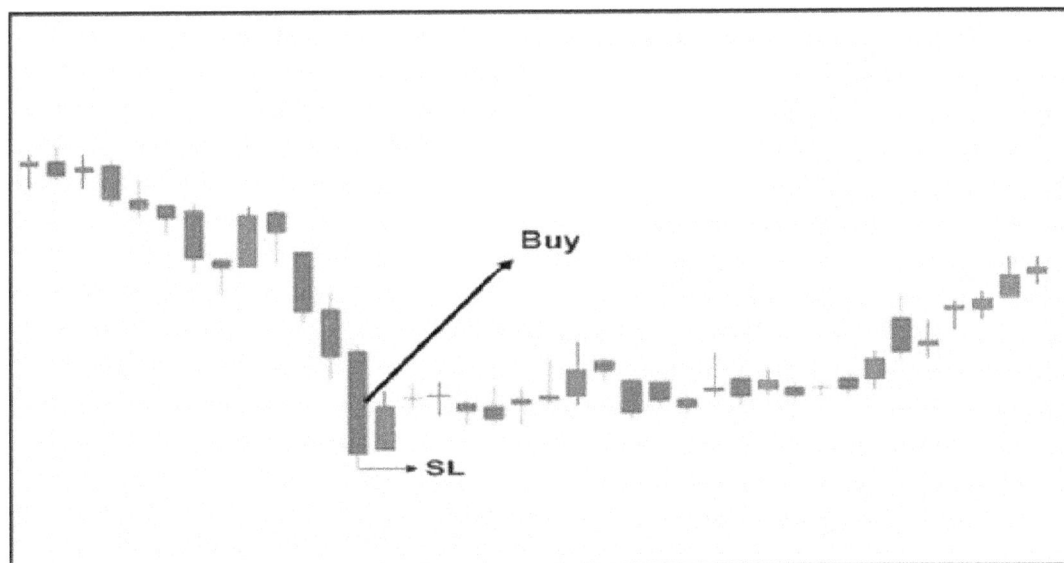

Strength of the Bullish Harami signal

The reversal signal is more reliable when the candles of the pattern are longer and also when the second candle closes up the first candle at a higher level.

Bearish Harami

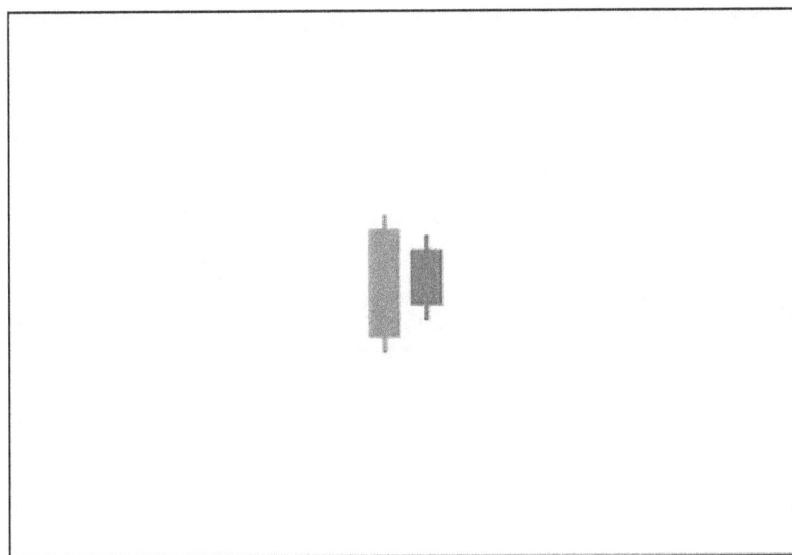

Formation:

- Bearish Harami is a bearish reversal pattern that occurs at the top of an uptrend or bullish price swing.

- First candle is white in line with the prevalent bullish trend.

- It has a large body indicating high level of buying interest.

- The second candle is black (bearish) and has a small body.

- The second candle's body completely lies within the body of the first candle.

Interpretation:

The first candle is bullish in line with the prevalent bullish trend indicating a heavy buying sentiment. But the next day market loses hope in the stock and lets the market open gap-down; trading on the stock takes place in a narrow range throughout the day. If the subsequent candle is black, bulls develop a sense of fear and give up, and price falls steadily and the Bearish Harami pattern gets validated.

Trading Bearish Harami

The midpoint of the white body or the last close (whichever is low) is the confirmation level. If price crosses below this level, it is a sell signal. The highest point of the pattern is the stop-loss.

However, while taking a sell decision based on a Bearish Harami pattern, one should always confirm that a resistance zone is nearby and a support zone is not near. Favorable movements of technical indicators like RSI and Stochastics reversing from overbought zone should also be a major positive factor for taking a sell decision.

Harami Cross

First candle is long and is moving in the direction of the trend. Second one is a doji.

The doji is within the body of the first candle.

Thus Harami Cross pattern is similar to the harami pattern except that the second candle in the case of a Harami Cross is a doji.

Presence of the doji indicates that trend reversal is probable.

The conditions to validate the Harami Cross pattern are the same as for a normal Harami pattern.

Harami Cross candlestick pattern is more reliable than a normal Harami pattern.

Harami Cross pattern can be a Bullish Harami Cross pattern or a Bearish Harami Cross pattern. Both the patterns are dealt with below.

Bullish Harami Cross

This pattern is called as Bullish Pregnant Cross also. This is a bullish reversal pattern that occurs at the bottom of a downtrend.

- First candle is black and long which indicates that sellers are in control of the market.

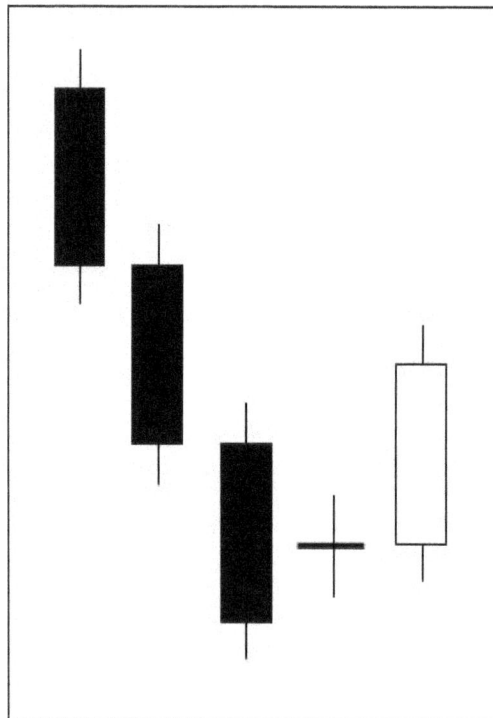

- Second candle is a doji which implies that market is now indecisive, that is, traders are not getting adequate information to decide whether to go long or to go short.

- The doji is completely within the body (range) of the first candle which means that activity in the market is less than the normal.

Interpretation

The first candle indicates that downtrend is prevailing in the stock. On the doji day, price opens higher than the previous close and steadily rises. This disappoints short-sellers who tend to buy to cover their short positions. The price rises further and the bullish pattern gets validated.

It can be observed from the above that this pattern resembles Morning Doji Star pattern in formation as well as implication.

Trading Bullish Harami Cross

Traders are not supposed to act on the occurrence of this pattern unless one or two subsequent candles are bullish and the price rises above the open of the first candle. The lowest point of the pattern will be the stop-loss.

However, while taking a buy decision based on a Bullish Harami Cross pattern, one should always confirm that support zone is nearby and resistance zone is not near. Favorable movements of technical indicators like RSI and Stochastics reversing from oversold zone should also be a major positive factor for buying.

Bearish Harami Cross

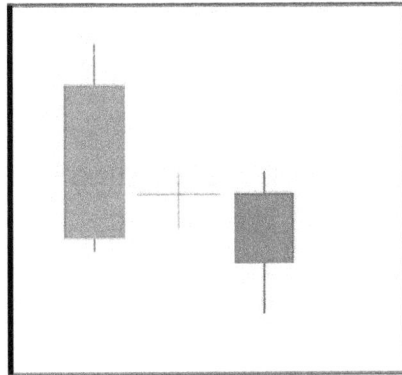

This pattern is called as Bearish Pregnant Cross also.

- This bearish reversal pattern occurs at the top of an uptrend.

- First candle is white and long indicating that buyers are in control of the market.

- Second candle is a doji which implies that market is now indecisive, that is, traders are not getting adequate information to decide whether to go long or to go short.

- The doji is completely within the body of the previous candle which means that the doji opened above the previous session's close and closed near the open.

Interpretation

Market's prevalent trend is uptrend. Market witnesses high level of buying activity as indicated by the large white body. But the next day buyers begin to doubt the sustainability of the upward momentum in the market because of lack of adequate information about the impending movement of the stock; price opens below the close of the prior day, trade takes place in a small range with less-than-normal volume throughout the session and closes at or near the open forming the doji If the subsequent candles close in black, the bearish pattern gets confirmed.

Trading the Bearish Harami Cross

A sell can be considered if price falls below the midpoint of the first candle or the last close. The highest point of the candlestick pattern will be the stop-loss.

However, while taking a sell decision based on Bearish Harami Cross pattern, one should always confirm that resistance zone is nearby and support zone is not near. Favorable movements of technical indicators like RSI and Stochastics reversing from overbought zone should also be a major positive factor for taking a sell decision.

Trading based on Harami patterns should be undertaken only when the price touches lower/upper Bollinger Band.

There is no way to fix profit targets objectively for trades based on Harami patterns. One may, therefore, take recourse to Fibonacci extensions/retracements or leave it to trailing stop loss or fix at the nearest support/resistance.

8. Morning Star & Morning Doji Star

Morning Star

As guessed by you correctly, the Morning Star is a sign of hope and indicates the dawn of a positive trend after a downtrend.

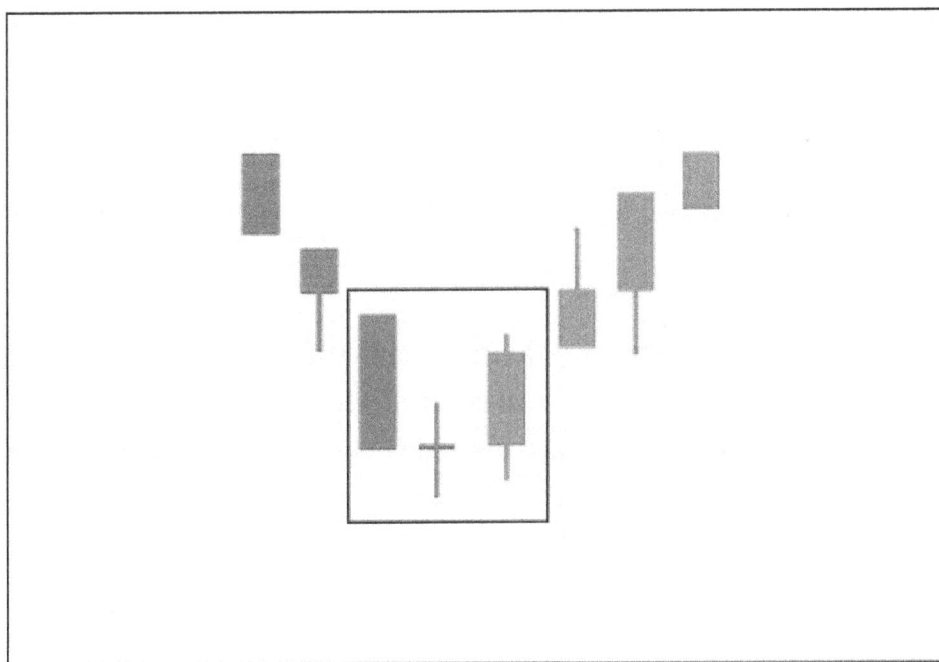

Formation

- The pattern is comprised of three candles and occurs at the bottom of a downtrend.

- First candle is long and is bearish in consonance with the prevailing downtrend.

- Second candle is a small-bodied candle. It can be a doji or a spinning top. That is, the second candle is indicating a condition of indecision prevailing at the market.

- The second candle's color is immaterial. That is, the second candle can be either white or black.

- The second candle appears outside the body of the first candle, i.e., gap down from the first candle.

- The third candle is long and white (bullish) and closes at least 50% up the first candle.

  To be brief, Morning Star candlestick pattern consists of three candles- a bearish candle followed by a small bullish or bearish candle, which is followed by a bullish candle that is larger than half of the first candle.

What does the pattern convey?

During the first candle's session, market continued to be controlled by bears as in the previous period. During the early session of the second (small-bodied) candle's session, market was under the control of bears but a state of indecision set in the minds of both the bulls and bears as to the market's future trend, and bears did not have the strength to bring down the price any longer, and the selling pressure started subsiding. This is the first indication that bulls may take control of the market. With the third candle which is long and white (bullish) and which opened gap-up the second candle and closed above the midpoint of the first candle, the down move is about to reverse and the bullish reversal of trend is about to come true.

How to trade

Though many traders are for buying above the first candle, I usually look for buying when the price rises above the high of the pattern, i.e., above the close of the last candle.

Stop Loss level

Though many traders place stop-loss orders below the lowest point in the pattern, i.e., below the middle candle, I recommend placing stop-loss below the real body of the middle candle as the former plan will entail a large gap between the buy order level and the stop loss level.

Signal strength

- Trend reversal will be more certain and stronger if the first candle and the last candle are long.

- The extent of the last candle's body covering the first candle's body shows the strength of the signal of reversal.

Morning Doji Star

Morning Doji Star pattern is quite similar to the Morning Star candlestick pattern except that the body of the second candle in the case of the Morning Doji Star is non-existent or extremely small.

Let us define the Morning Doji Star in the usual way as follows:

Morning Star Doji pattern is a 3-candlestick formation occurring at the bottom of a downtrend indicating a major bullish reversal. It is comprised of a long black candlestick followed by a doji that gaps down from the first candle. Third candle is a long white candle that closes above the middle of the first candle.

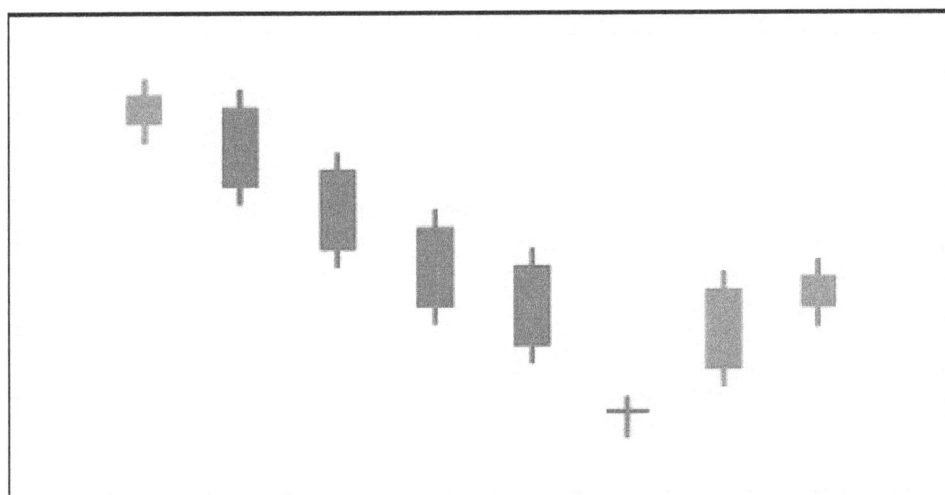

The psychology behind the pattern

The first candle is in downtrend in tune with the prevailing trend. The second day witnesses further fall in price and a doji forms with a gap down indicating that the day is still in the grip of bears. But the narrow gap between the open and close encourages bulls the next day; bears start covering their shorts, and market trend starts reversing from the downtrend to uptrend.

How to trade

Buy when the price crosses above the last close of the pattern. Stop loss will be the lowest level of the pattern.

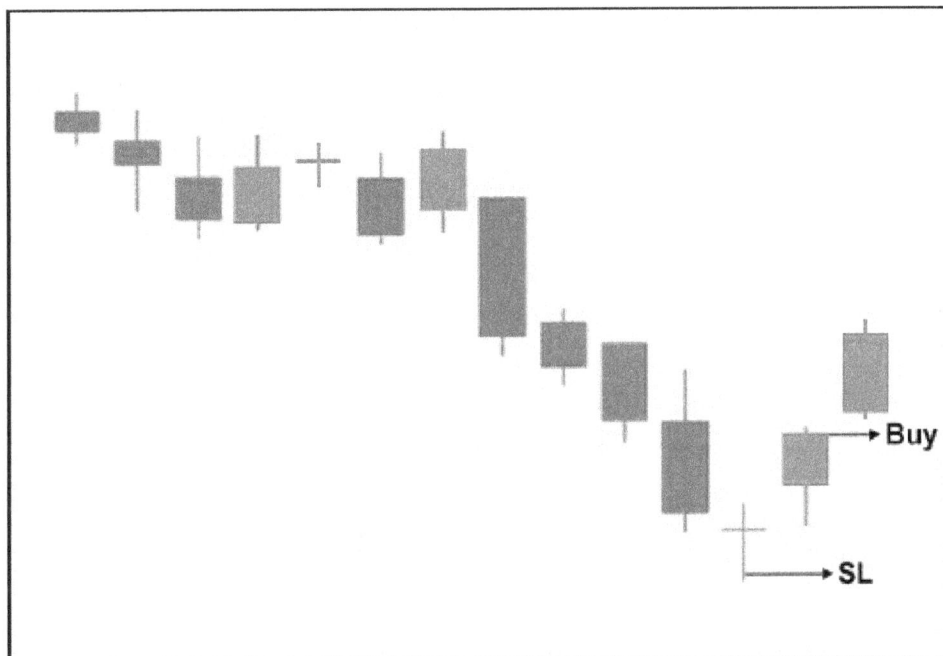

Stop loss will be the lowest level of the pattern.

9. Evening Star & Evening Doji Star

Evening Star

The evening star is the exact opposite of the morning star; it occurs at the top of an uptrend and signals that a downtrend is about to occur.

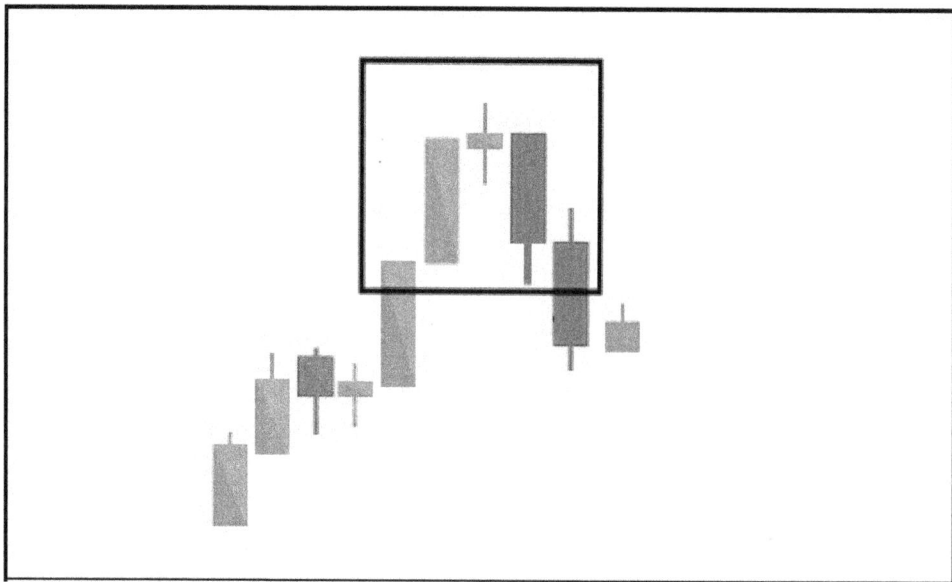

Formation:

- The first candle is a long-bodied bullish candle.

- The second candle's body is small; it opens gap-up from the first candle; it can be white or black.

- The third candle is a long bearish candlestick that passes at least halfway down the first bullish candle i.e., closes well within the first candle's real body.

The psychology behind the pattern

1. Initially buyers were in control of the market and were pushing the price up.

2. Then market became indecisive with buyers and sellers not having sufficient clue as to the future trend of price; this led to the small-bodied second candle with a gap up in tune with the previous candle's direction.

3. Then sellers became dominant in the market and brought down the price and buyers started booking profit.

How to trade

Go short when the price breaks below 50% of the first candle. Place stop-order a little above the real body of the second candle.

Signal strength

Trend reversal will be more forceful when the Evening Star pattern has gaps. A gap up between the first and the second candles and a gap down between the second candle and the third candle will be more likely followed by a trend reversal.

Trend reversal will be more forceful when the first and the third candles are long.

The more the third candle erases the gains of the first candle, the stronger the trend reversal will be.

According to Bulkowski, the Evening Star pattern predicts a fall in prices with an accuracy rate of 72%.

Evening Doji Star

- Evening Doji Star is a bearish reversal pattern that occurs at the top of an uptrend.

- It is comprised of 3 candles.

- First candle is long and white.

- Second candle is a doji that gaps up from the first day's close.

- Third candle is a long black candle whose closing price is within the first day's white body.

In other words, if the second candle of an Evening Star pattern is a doji candle, the pattern is called an "Evening Doji Star".

Below is an example of an Evening Doji Star:

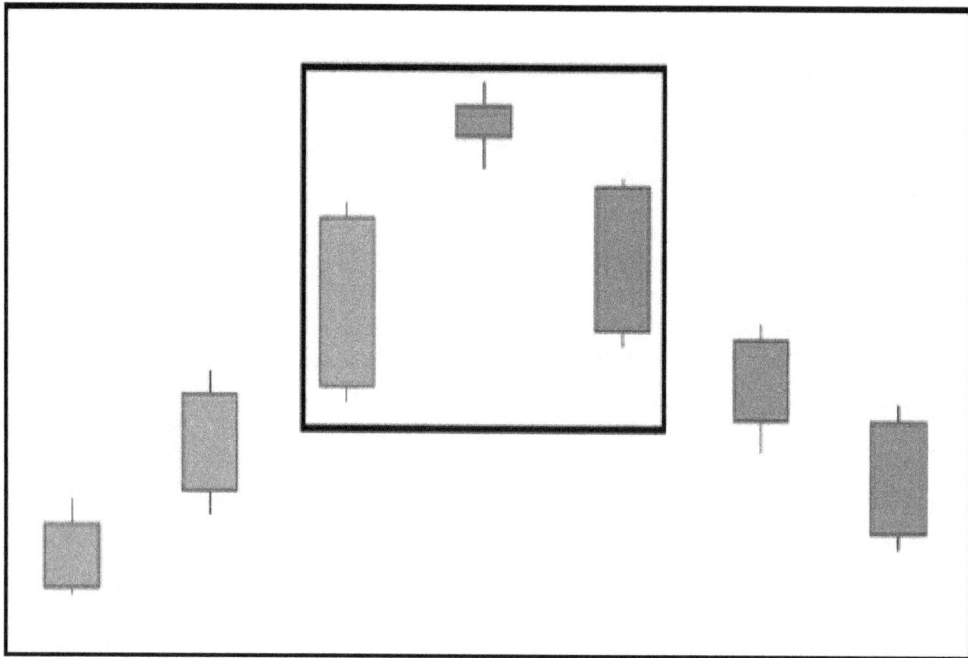

The Evening Doji Star is considered to be a stronger signal than the Evening Star as the former pattern's middle candle is a doji.

Strength of the signal of the pattern

The more the third candle covers the first candle's body, the more forceful is the pattern's signal of bearish reversal.

How to trade

Sell when price crosses below the last close.

Place stop loss at a little above the doji candle.

10. Dark Cloud Cover

The name "Dark Cloud Cover" itself hints that it must be a bearish reversal pattern – a black cloud formed over the previous day's uptrend.

Formation of the pattern

- First candle is white and mostly long.

- Second candle is black and mostly long.

- The second candle opens strongly above the previous candle's high but subsequently declines and closes within the previous candle and below the midpoint of the previous candle's body.

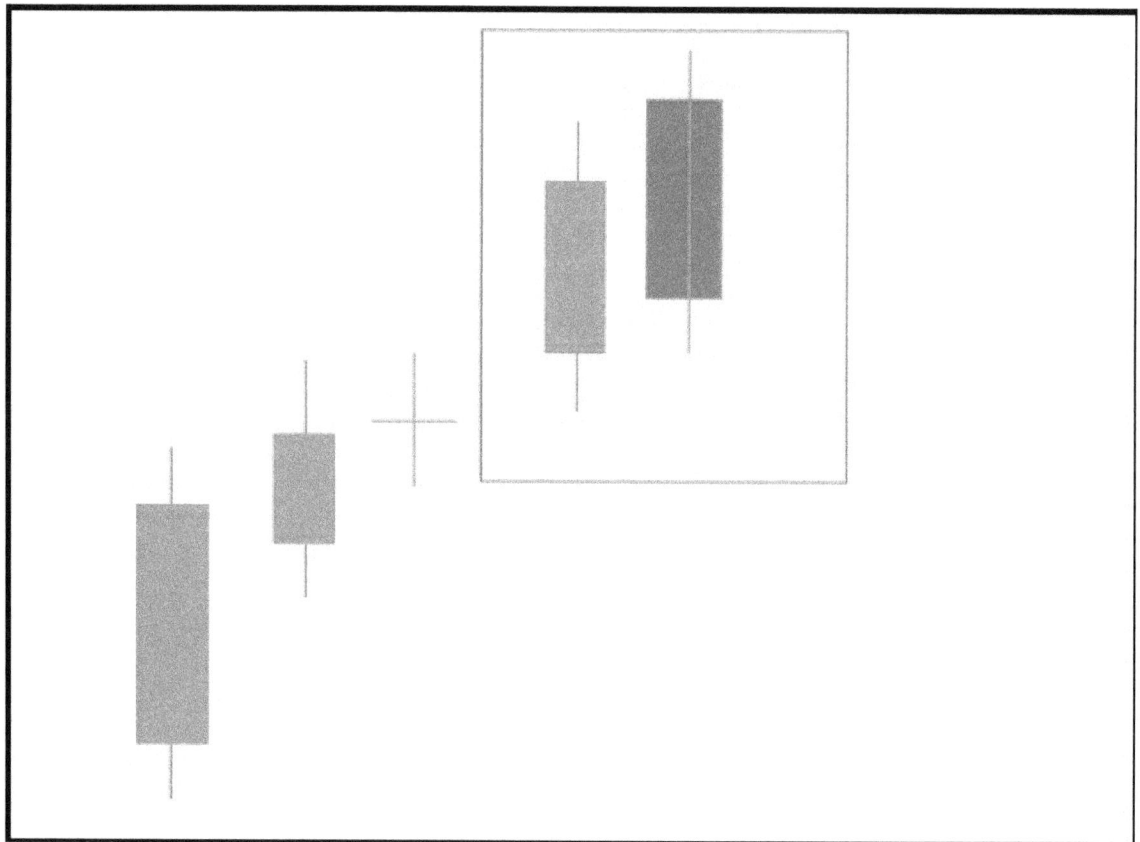

Interpretation of the Dark Cloud Cover Pattern

Currently market is in strong uptrend as seen from the first candle which is white and long. Appearance of the second candle which is black and long alerts that bears are now dominating the session and are pushing the prices downward thus bringing the uptrend to an end.

How to trade

One may sell or go short when price falls below the last close.

Stop loss could be the highest point of the entire formation.

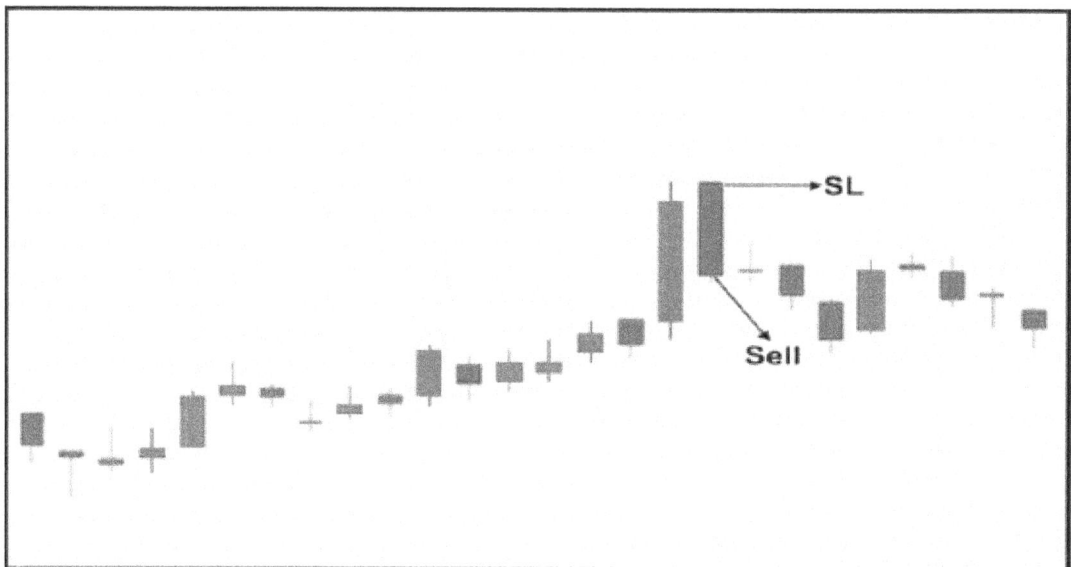

Traders use this pattern mostly to get alert to exit from the long position to avert or minimize loss due to falling prices.

Signal strength

- Increased volume during these sessions will confirm the strength of the reversal signal.

- The longer the real bodies of the white candle and the black candle, the stronger the reversal signal will be.

- The higher the gap up by the second candle from the first candle close, the stronger the reversal signal will be.

- The lower the second candle crosses below the first candle, the stronger the reversal signal will be.

Resemblance to other candlestick patterns:

- Dark Cloud Cover pattern resembles the Bearish Engulfing pattern; the difference between the two is that the second candle of the Bearish Engulfing Pattern opens above the close of the first candle while Dark Cloud Cover pattern does not completely engulf the first candle and its second candle opens above the high of the first candle and closes below the midpoint of first candle's body.

- Piercing Line pattern is exactly the reverse of the Dark Cloud Cover.

- Bearish Meeting Lines is similar to the Dark Cloud Cover; the difference between the two is that in the case of Bearish Meeting Lines, the second candle which is long and black closes at or near the same price that the white candle had closed.

11. Piercing Line

Piercing Line is a two-candle bullish reversal pattern that occurs in downtrends or during a pullback within an uptrend, or at the support. The first candlestick is long and bearish. The second candlestick opens below the closing level of the first one i.e., gap down and closes more than halfway (preferably two-thirds of the way) into the first candle's real body. Both bodies should be long enough. Thus it depicts a strong recovery of the previous day's losses and commencement of a bullish trend.

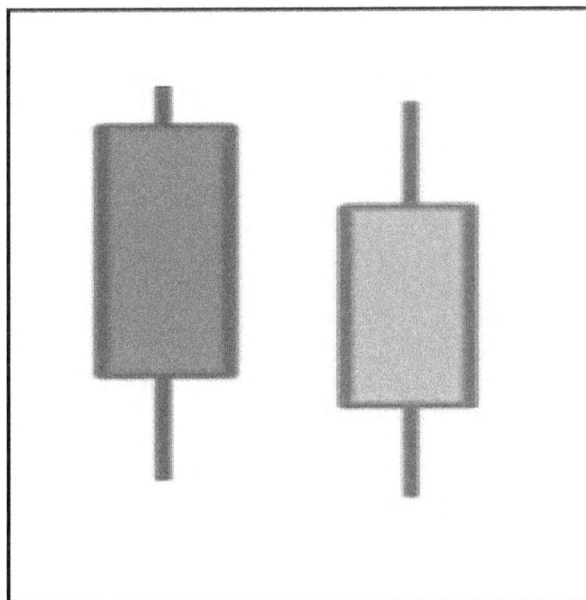

Interpretation of the pattern

If a very big change happens in a single candle's session, it is an indication that a big change in market direction is taking place. Such a big change occurs generally as a result of important news that has bearing on the fundamentals of the company, industry or economy like earnings report, incidence of new taxes and securing of major supply order. Let us see how this condition develops:

Initially sellers are in so much control of the market that they can push the market down to close in black. The next day market opens gap-down in tune with the existing downtrend. But after the opening of the market, bullish sentiment takes over bearish sentiment due to release of some news like good earnings report or winning of tender; market turning positive. Bears get fear and rush to cover their short positions which further strengthens the buying forces leading to rally in prices.

Bullish Engulfing Pattern Vs. Piercing Line

Like Bullish Engulfing pattern, the pattern Piercing Line also succeeds in amazingly rising after a downtrend and a gap down. But this pattern could rise only to a level of half of the previous black candle's body while a Bullish Engulfing pattern rises and closes higher than the opening of the previous black candle. Thus we can understand that the Bullish Engulfing pattern is a more powerful bullish indicator than a Piercing Line pattern.

Dark Cloud Cover Vs. Piercing Line

The Piercing Line pattern is the exact opposite of the Dark Cloud Cover. Piercing Line is a bullish reversal pattern and the Dark Cloud Cover is a bearish reversal pattern.

How to trade

One can enter into buy trade after prices cross above the last close. Conservative traders wait till the third candle closes above the pattern high i.e., the first candle's high, and enter trade the next day at the open. The lowest point of the candlestick pattern is recommended as stop-loss.

Determinants of the signal strength of the pattern

- The larger the candles in the pattern, the stronger the trend reversal.

- The larger the volumes on the two sessions, the higher the probability of reversal.

- The deeper the gap down at the opening of the second session, the stronger the trend reversal.

- The higher the second candle covers the body of the first candle, the stronger the reversal.

12. Belt Hold

Bullish Belt Hold - Formation

Bullish Belt Hold is a long white candlestick without a lower shadow (a bullish Morubozu) occurring after a black candle in a downtrend. It opens lower than the low of the previous candle; the open is the low of the day. It rallies against the current downtrend and closes near its high and within the body of the previous candle.

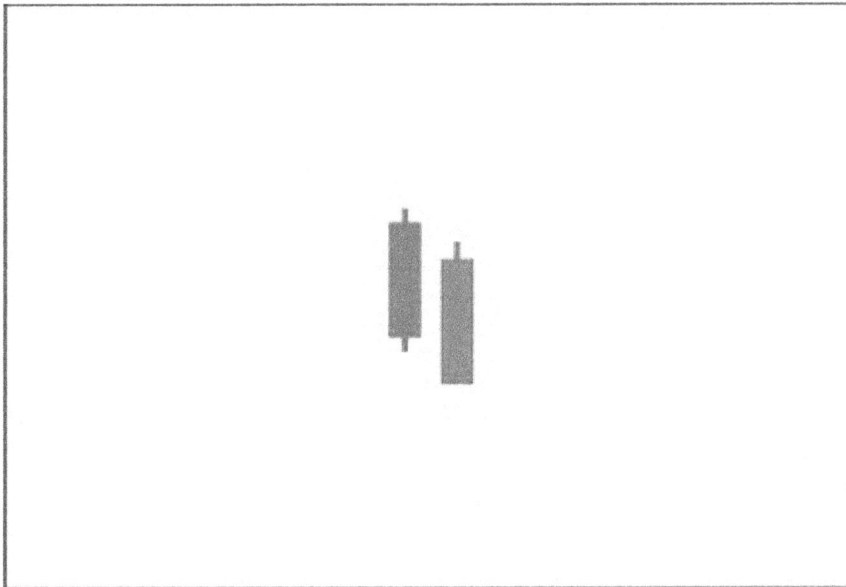

Interpretation of the pattern

The pattern displays a session where bulls became so strong that market moved in a single direction with no going back.

How to trade

One can consider buying when the market crosses above the last close. Stop loss will be the pattern low.

Strength of The Reversal Signal of The Pattern

The longer the body of the white candle, the stronger is the reversal signal.

Bearish Belt Hold–Formation

Bearish Belt Hold is a black Morubozu that occurred after a white candle in an uptrend. It opened higher than the high of the previous candle, and its open was the high of the day. During the day it fell steadily against the overall trend of the market and closed near its low and within the body of the previous candle. The candle never traded higher than the opening price and naturally, it had no upper shadow.

Interpretation of the pattern

The market opens gap-up in the direction of the prevailing uptrend but it is moving in the opposite direction creating fear in the minds of bulls; the bulls start covering their long positions which adds to the bearish sentiment and leads to formation of black Morubozu.

How to trade

Traders can consider selling/short selling when the market falls below the last close. However, traders are advised to wait for the market to test the pattern instead of entering into trade as soon as the belt hold pattern appears.

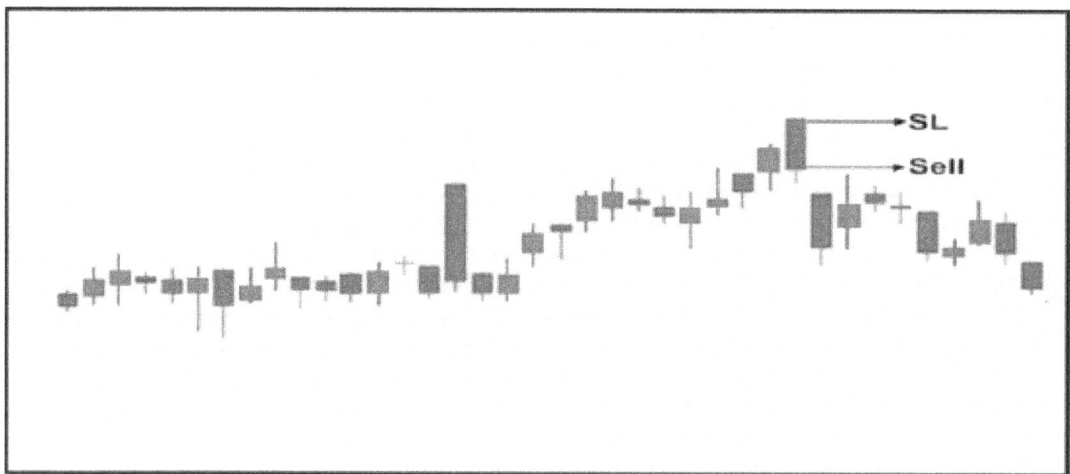

Stop loss will be the pattern high.

Strength of the reversal signal of the Belt Hold Pattern

Bullish Belt Hold pattern predicts the occurrence of bullish reversal in 71% of the occasions and the Bearish Belt Hold pattern predicts trend reversal in 68% of the occasions.

13. Three White Soldiers

Formation:

- The pattern is comprised of three consecutive, long white candles.

- Each candle opens within the previous candle's body, ideally a little below the previous close or at least above the middle of the previous candle's body.

- Each candle closes at its high or near its high.

- Each candle closes at a new high i.e., each candle's closing price is higher than the closing price of the previous candle.

All the above characteristics imply that buying pressure is steadily increasing.

Three White Soldiers pattern acts as a bullish reversal pattern if it occurs at the bottom of a downtrend and as a continuation pattern if it occurs during a consolidation phase in an uptrend.

And by this time you would have found that the Three White Soldiers pattern is the opposite of the Three Black Crows pattern.

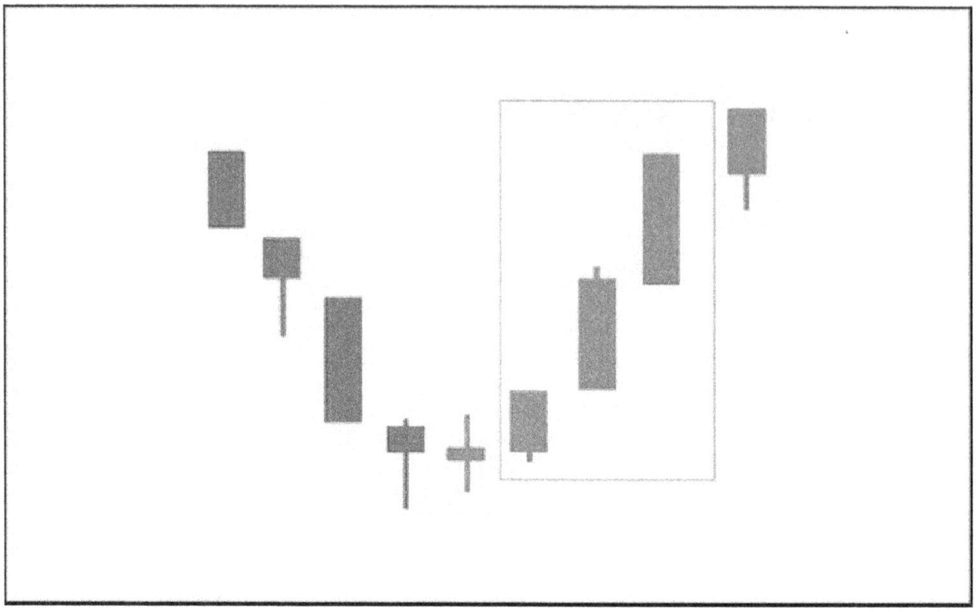

Interpretation of the pattern

If the pattern occurs at the bottom of a downtrend or during a period of stable prices, it implies that traders' sentiment has changed and the minor pullback is over and the previous trend is likely to resume. This causes fear among the bears who now consider exiting their short positions which will again add acceleration to rise in prices.

How to trade

Buying after prices cross the last close is recommended.

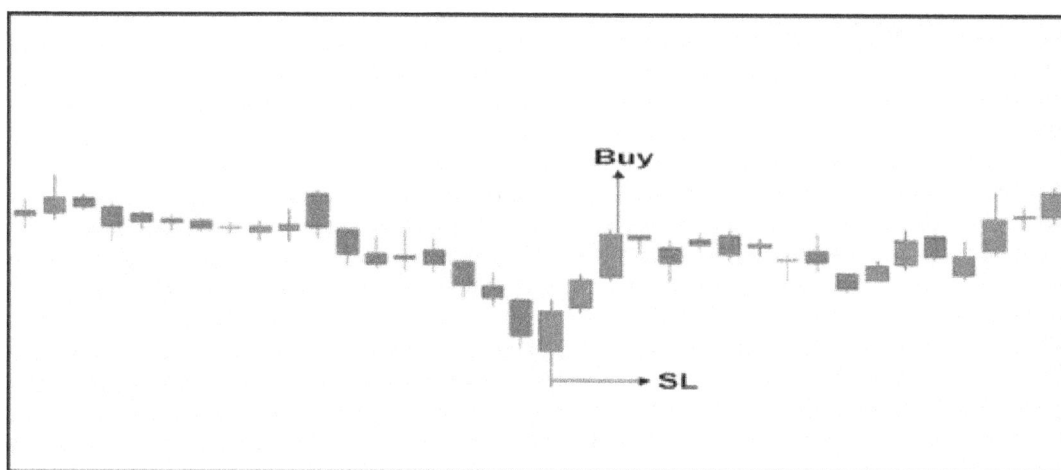

However, we cannot take it for granted that the Three White Soldiers pattern is a bullish reversal pattern. The formation can be a reversal pattern if it takes place after a long downtrend. If the formation occurs after a small pullback that has happened during an ongoing uptrend, the pattern will be a continuation pattern only in which case traders can wait before going long.

Likewise, the steep and continuous increase in prices caused by three consecutive bullish candles could take the stock/tradable asset to overbought level and prices may turn to a breather and may undergo a pullback before resuming the bullish move.

We may, therefore, buy If the formation is confirmed as a reversal pattern by positive indications like a gap-up or a long white candle and surge in volume.

Stop loss may be placed at the lowest point of the pattern.

14. Three Black Crows

Three black crows is a highly reliable candlestick pattern that predicts reversal of an uptrend. This pattern is the opposite of the Three White Soldiers formation. It is an easily identifiable pattern; there is no need for memorizing any formula or shortcut. The pattern simply consists of three black candles making a formation like stairs. Each of the three candles opens within the body of the preceding candle and closes lower than the preceding candle. The formation signals that the ongoing uptrend is weakening and reversal of the trend is likely.

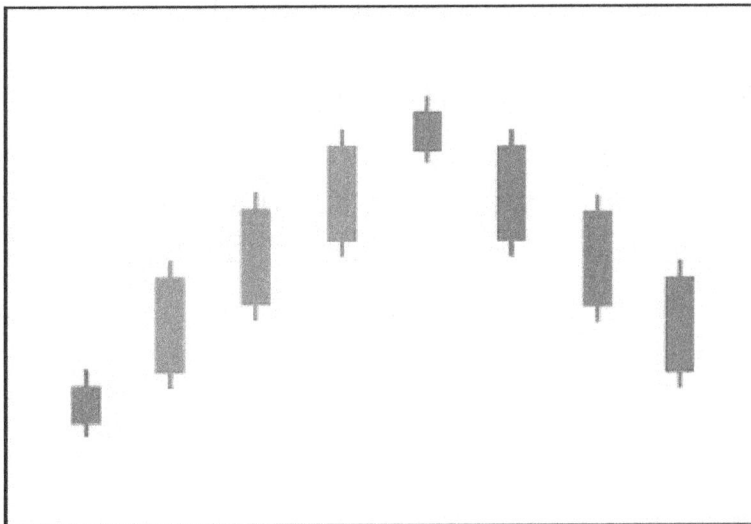

Formation of the pattern in detail

- Market is on uptrend.

- Three consecutive black and slightly long candlesticks appear at the top of the uptrend.

- Each candlestick opens within the body of the previous candlestick, preferably below the middle of the body of the previous candlestick. In other words, the opening price of each candle is higher than the previous candle's close.

- Each candlestick closes at a new low. That is, the second candle does not break the high of the first candle and the third candle does not break the high of the second candle

- The third candlestick's body and the second candlestick's body are of the same size or the third candle's body is a little larger.

- Lower shadows are absent or very short.

In essence, Three Black Crows pattern is formed when prices fall for three consecutive days because of the weakening of the ongoing uptrend; reversal of the uptrend is likely.

The psychology behind the pattern

Each day witnesses price falling below the low of the preceding day. It means that buyers are not optimistic and are closing their long positions and bears get stronger enough to push down prices.

How to trade Three Black Crows pattern

Sell if price falls below the last close.

Place stop loss level at a little above the high of the pattern.

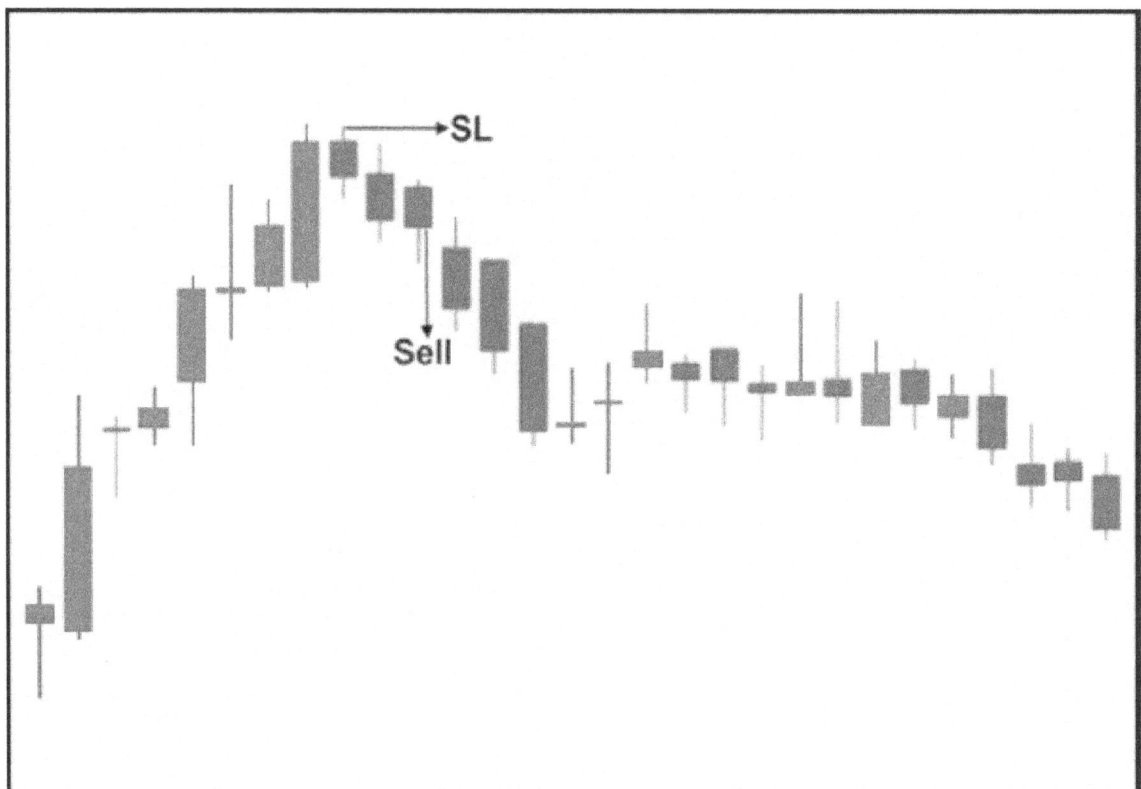

However take confirmation by other indicators like support & resistance zones, moving averages and oversold readings like RSI above 70 before trading as the three black candles could have led to oversold condition and could, therefore, undergo consolidation phase before resuming downtrend. It must be kept in mind that these three candles can be a Bearish Morubozu also.

Strength of the signal of Three Black Crows pattern

The bearish trend should be confirmed by the subsequent candle being bearish, opening gap-down or closing lower.

According to Bulkowski, the Three Black Crows pattern predicts falling prices with an accuracy rate of 78%.

However, the pattern's accuracy level of prediction of trend reversal depends on how well the pattern has formed. The bigger the candles' real bodies, the more accurate the pattern's prediction of falling market. That is, the shorter the lower shadows, the more accurate the pattern's prediction of falling market. The higher the volume of trading during the pattern, the more certain the decline in prices.

Conclusion

We learnt 14 highly accurate and frequently occurring candlestick patterns that signal trading opportunities. I am sure that you would have by this time got a clear idea as to how to identify those candlestick patterns. You would have understood that the best way of making trade decisions is to wait for the formation of a reliable candlestick pattern and find out whether the support and resistance levels, overbought and oversold zones and interaction of short-term and longer-term moving average curves are not contradictory to the trading signal of the candlestick patterns. You would have understood that if many technical indicators are all unanimous in buy-sell signals, the trade will have a high probability of success and one can boldly plunge into trading.

You are now adequately armed to trade candlestick patterns profitably. In the initial days of learning tcandlestick patterns, it is better to practise trading at a small scale whenever a tradable pattern is identified.

All the best!

www.ingramcontent.com/pod-product-compliance
Lightning Source LLC
Chambersburg PA
CBHW061326190326
41458CB00011B/3906